Growing Carnations

Growing Carnations

Second Edition

Joy Jarratt

Kangaroo Press

Acknowledgements

Information on the history of carnations was obtained from *The Royal Horticultural Society's Book on Gardening*.

For lists of carnations and relevant information, the following people came to my rescue:

Grow West, Munster, Western Australia
George, Two Wells, South Australia
Daly's Flowers, Murray Bridge, South Australia
F and I Baguley, Clayton Sth, Victoria
Graeme Guy, Plant Pathologist, Victoria

Paul Rumkorf, Victoria
Max Cutler, Sydney
Parklands Flowers, Queensland
Elizabeth Minchinton, Institute of Horticultural Development, Victoria
Megan Hill, Institute of Horticultural Development, Victoria (for information on western flower thrip)

None of these people are in any way associated with what I have written, since they have not seen the script, and are not responsible for my interpretation of their information.

Camera

I use a Minolta SLR 101T which is a fairly old but reliable camera. A Plus 3 filter was used to get close enough to the subject.

Shots were taken by a hand-held camera in natural light as flash distorted the delicate colours of some of the blooms. Wind and movement were always a problem. The cardboard backdrop was used as a contrast to the colour of the blooms; many carnations were photographed with both black and aqua backing and the best photo, or the one with the most natural colour, was used. Some had to be photographed where they were growing.

Generally Kodak 64 ASA film was used.

Cover picture: 'Rendevous'

First published in 1988 by Kangaroo Press Pty Ltd
Second edition published by Kangaroo Press in 1996
3 Whitehall Road, Kenthurst NSW 2156 Australia
PO Box 6125 Dural Delivery Centre NSW 2158
Printed in Hong Kong through Colorcraft Ltd

ISBN 0 86417 817 4

Contents

Introduction

The old-fashioned carnation will always be a popular flower with the home gardener. They are excellent as cut flowers on account of their fragrance and long-lasting qualities, and are adaptable, vigorous growers, even in coastal or mountainous areas. Furthermore, international competition in the last ten years has advanced the range, size, and quality of carnations, bringing a big following in the cut flower market.

Extreme weather, especially in winter affects the quality and quantity of blooms; high temperatures often reduce the blooms to a smaller size, while winter rains and cold increase the incidence of damaged flowers and disease. Often blooms do not open completely in cold weather. This is just the effect of sudden changes in the weather; carnations will bloom comfortably in either winter or summer; it is a sudden rise or fall in temperature that does the damage.

Commercial growers avoid these problems by using plastic igloo hot houses, planting their cultivars as close as 10 cm apart. This of course is too close for the home gardener. In commercial situations watering and fertilisers are measured and applied by an automatically controlled mechanism. The average gardener does not have the equipment for this intensive culture.

This book is not intended for the commercial grower, for whom adequate information is available elsewhere, but for the amateur gardener, for whom information is scarce. I have been growing carnations for 34 years now, and compiled this book from notes taken over that period, hoping my observations and experiments will be of assistance to other growers.

To grow a carnation is to learn to love them. Their perfume, grace and beauty and long-lasting qualities make them the most rewarding flower for the efforts of the gardener. To love them is to want to possess the newest tantalising tones, and with the new genetic engineering, all colours are possible.

I have recently visited carnation farms in the eastern states. The progress made in breeding better quality blooms with stronger perfume and a wider variety of colours, will soon bring carnations back into vogue. Flowers are now big business, and with the cloning and genetic engineering available to make the cut blooms last longer, there will be considerable spin-off for the home gardener.

Carnations now range from the Gipsy variety, the size and form of Sweet William, mini micro, micro, a variety of pinks, dianthus, a big variety of sprays to borders and standard blooms. The range is monumental.

There are very few problems with growing carnations if they are cultivated properly. Usually a poor or diseased plant is the fault of the grower and due to lack of care.

History

The carnation, or *Dianthus caryophyllus* for the botanically minded, originally had its home in central and southern Europe and Asia. It was known in the hills of the Mediterranean as dianthus, the divine flower of the gods. All varieties of carnations and pinks grown today have been bred from the species which originated in these areas. It found its way into English and then American gardens, where it has been cultivated and interbred to the fine specimens we have today.

As early as 1629 an Englishman named Parkinson wrote of the carnation that its bravery, variety and sweet smell joined together, made everyone eager to grow or acquire it. Even at that date the carnation was known in several varieties, for in gardens in England and on the Continent it varied in habit and stature, size and colour, with single and double petals in different forms. The wild plants had a distinctly saw-toothed or notched edge, some were of more distinct perfume than others; and so in the course of time several well-marked classes evolved.

Like most other flowers the carnation has had its ups and downs in popularity. A hundred and twenty years ago the Border carnation was so favoured by flower growers in England that many local flower shows were devoted to it exclusively. Then with the introduction of pelargoniums and lobelias, it declined for a while, though it was never entirely neglected.

The carnation began to revive again in the 1880s and to regain some of its old popularity, but the great impetus which resulted in the present enthusiasm for this flower occurred in 1895, when a Mr Peter Fisher of Ellis, Massachusetts, raised the deep rose-pink variety 'Mrs T.W. Lawson' by crossing 'Daybreak' with 'Van Leeuwen'. Something of a sensation was caused by the purchase of stock from this variety by Mr Thomas W. Lawson, a copper magnate, for a great sum of well over two thousand pounds. This variety was the forerunner of the Perpetual Flowering race that is now grown in such massive quantities for the market and in private gardens today.

Tall growing Remontant carnations were grown in France as early as 1750. They were different in stature from Border carnations and required no period of rest. These were imported into England and America in the middle of the nineteenth century, but it was some time before cross breeding produced the varieties with strong stems and calyces and lasting petals, and which flowered freely over the winter period, which have evolved into the Perpetual Flowering carnations of today.

Remontant carnations did not oust the Border carnations nor find much favour with the old florists who valued form and colour above other assets. These carnations were not allowed to flower in the first year and sometimes not in the second, but grown in large bushes or trained on the roof of the bush or hot house in which they were grown. On the whole, even in the more compact varieties such as 'A. Alegatiere', which received a first-class certificate in 1877, they found less favour than might have been expected.

The strong variety 'Mrs T.W. Lawson' brought the stronger stems, strong calyces, lasting petals and free-flowering habit extending over the winter period, which the best of the Tree carnations such as 'William Robinson' lacked. Very soon came ' Mrs H. Burnett' and 'Britannia', and no year since has failed to see additions to the Perpetual Flowering varieties available to growers around the world.

Just as the Perpetual Flowering carnation had its origin in the French Remontant carnation, so had the Malmaison class. The Blush 'Souvenir de Malmaison' was raised in France in 1857 as a seedling from the Remontant form and was so named for its likeness to the rose 'Souvenir de Malmaison'. The Perpetual Malmaisons similarly arose as seedlings from the early Perpetual Flowering carnations about 1903.

Through the crossing of Border carnations, the intermediate type sometimes called the Perpetual Border carnation was established. Later, through crossing with the pink, the Perpetual Flowering carnations have had a part in the development of the race of pinks with the long flowering period known as Dianthus x 'Allwoodii', named after the firm of Messrs Allwood who originated and developed it.

In 1938 a Scotsman, William Sim, emigrated to America and raised a carnation that was far more free-flowering than previous varieties. This was the forerunner of the now very popular Sims, which have a tall growth habit and have been know to reach 1.5 metres high. Now Sims have been improved to a much stronger, longer-lasting, perfumed carnation and are used in laboratories for tissue culture, creating a multitude of new plants.

Israel, Spain, England, Holland, Germany, Brazil, U.S.A., Australia, Japan and New Zealand are all competing for sales of their newest carnations. I have looked at 16 brochures with an average of 70 different varieties per grower, each carnation having a different name; but many appeared the same. This is where the confusion comes in regarding a named variety. The Avonmore 'Candy' is pink. The Klemm of the same name is gold with a pink fleck. It is impossible to list all carnations in Australia, and many are available to flower growers only.

Modern Flower Culture

Genetic engineering of plants is a very competitive business, with a Melbourne-based company at the top of the list. Having already introduced the blue rose, they are improving carnations to double their vase life.

Genetic engineering is manipulating plants to be insect- and disease-resistant, while retaining form, colour and perfume. This is a long-term, risky and expensive undertaking. For this reason a patent is put on perfected cultivars, and they can be purchased only by commercial flower growers, after a binding contract has been signed. When a company spends $19 million on research, they must protect their investment.

New technology to double the vase life of a bloom, consists of transferring anti-ethylene genes into any carnation cultivar. (The deterioration of a bloom is triggered by ethylene.) Previous breeding techniques produced cultivars with improved vase life, often at the expense of colour and perfume. A range of preservatives is available to improve the vase life, but chemical additives are not environmentally friendly.

A number of carnation plants have been trialled, with white Sim the most advanced. Sale of these genetically engineered plants will be in Australia, Europe and the U.S.A. in the near future, when the patent for the technology is in place.

Genetic manipulation also involves the insertion of a colour gene creating blue-coloured flowers. The gene colouring from petunias will be trialled in carnations. This colour was successful in a rose, and it is expected violet, purple and lilac will follow.

Genetically modified plants possess antibiotic-resistant or herbicide-resistant genes. Roses so far have been the most trialled plants, but there are proposals for other plants. Transgenic tomato plants are available, bearing tomatoes which are able to ripen on the plant longer, giving them a better flavour and the ability to withstand transport damage. Transgenic cotton has been engineered to withstand the herbicide Roundup.

Following up on my research into carnations, I visited a friend in Monbulk to whom I had given some cuttings to many years ago. His interest is in Border carnations and dianthus. Paul Rumkorf took his research to the point of contacting growers in England and New Zealand, for information and seeds with the purpose of cross-pollinating.

He assures me 'Jon Cleary' is originally from the *Dianthus Allwoodii* strain, as is 'Juliet', 'London Smoke' and 'Freckles', but many of these old plants are lost in time. 'Jon Cleary' is proving to be an excellent cross-pollinator because of the plant's quality and strength.

Books dating back as far as the 1800s suggests the Border carnation had long arms for easy layering. Border carnations were then an untidy plant. I suggest this characteristic has been grown out over the years, to the more upright plants we have now. They have smooth-edged blooms on long stems.

Dianthus allwoodii, (the last name being dropped over the years, leading to the confusion as to the plant's background) has a variety of forms. Their size ranges from that of a 20-cent piece up to 6 cm across, with stems up to 50 cm. The fact that they are so easy to grow, with their high perfume rating makes them worth looking at. A border of good quality dianthus, the named perennial varieties, is a worthwhile investment for the gardener with little time to spare.

Seed has been gathered from old Border carnations and dianthus that have been growing for thirty years. These strains were cross-pollinated with strains from other countries, with some delightful results. It is hoped these new varieties will reach the market in a year or so.

Classes

There are many different classes of carnation on the market, and generally the same conditions suit them all. So if you have had a bed of seed dianthus that did not give an abundance of flowers, it would be quite unrealistic to expect Border or another type of carnation to do well in the same spot. While a commercial grower will usually stick to the same type or class, there is an interesting variety to choose from, each one having a special attraction of its own.

I have in the same bed Sims and Avonmore which are Perpetual Flowering carnations, along with the hardier American Spray and Border carnations and some pinks. The selection is only the result of my being attracted to the colour or the particular perfume, which varies with the individual type. Most of these have been interbred over the years making it difficult to tell their origins. Perpetual Flowering carnations will flower all the year around; in the other classes some are perpetual while others in the same class may flower only in the spring or summer.

Seed carnations and dianthus will take 28 and 20 weeks respectively to flower and may be accurately timed to suit the grower, provided conditions on the seed packet are adhered to.

Standard or Perpetual Flowering Carnations

With a little care Perpetual Flowering carnations will bloom all year around. They are not as hardy as the Border carnation but will continue to bloom in the garden if conditions are not too severe. A windbreak of plastic can be the easiest means of protection in winter. They do well in a glasshouse if well ventilated, for they require airy conditions and a rather dry atmosphere, and do best if some distance from the glass. An ideal night temperature of 10°C would keep the plants happy. They grow well in pots and are useful grown this way for house decoration.

There is a wide choice of colours, with markings or plain, and the edges of the petals may be smooth, fringed or picoted. The flowers have a well-formed calyx with a well-built centre.

11

Flower stems will be strong and whippy and up to 70 cm long even in home gardens, if suitably protected from the wind. Flowers should be 8 cm across with petals long, broad and substantial, especially the outer or guard petals which should rise perpendicularly a good centimetre above the calyx, then spread gracefully in a horizontal direction; the inner petals should diminish gradually in size, filling but not crowding the centre of the flower. All the petals should be regularly disposed and lie over each other so their respective colour and design should meet the eye all together. They should be nearly flat or only slightly inflexed at the broad end; their edges should be perfectly entire, without notch, fringe or indenture.

The calyx should be at least 2.5 cm long and sufficiently strong at the top to keep the bases of the petals in a strong circular body. The middle of the flower should not rise too high above the other parts. The colour should be bright and equally marked all over the flower. The stripes should be regular, narrowing gradually to the claw of the petal and there ending in a fine point.

Spray Carnations

Spray carnations are now almost as popular as the Standards. The development of Sprays over the last ten years, has brought them to their peak, some of them being as large as a medium Standard. Most sprays may be disbudded to attain one larger bloom, but you lose some of the ongoing blossom effect, which adds to the charm of Sprays.

Many Sprays are a smaller version of a Standard, the name being different. A Spray, if fed correctly can have up to 25 blooms per stem. As one bloom fades, pick it out and allow the next bud room to burst. The range of colours and the quality of the new Sprays makes them worthwhile considering. For anyone who loves carnations, yet finds the Standards too much work, I suggest you look at the Sprays. You will not be disappointed. Where there are several blooms on a stem they will all be smaller than if only one bud had been allowed to develop.

To grow these carnations is less work as they only need to be 'stopped' once and are not disbudded as frequently. The well-grown and vigorous young plants will produce 'breaks' or shoots at each node quite frequently. These carnations are extremely suitable for growing in pots and are excellent for cut flowers in the house as buds will develop and open even after the first bud has withered, if dead buds are removed and water is changed regularly.

Border Carnations

Border carnations are strong growing and never need 'stopping' as the plant has a tendency to be bushy which becomes more marked after the second season. Generally they bloom in spring and summer, with a flower that is flat and open, the true Old English show class flower. Border carnations are not as readily available for purchase as the Perpetual Flowering varieties which are propagated on a commercial basis and do sell well. However it is a pity more Border carnations are not publicised as they are the easiest to manage, need no staking and give an abundance of exquisite blooms with a lasting bouquet.

Research suggests it was the Dutch who first introduced the Bizarres, Flakes, and Picotees, which were all originally Border carnations. With the race for better and more colourful blooms, these were all interbred over the years. Many Borders and Sprays will flower all the year around with proper care. Few growers still have a supply of Borders, as the Standard and Spray carnations are more popular. But the Borders have a charm of their own, with one grower cultivating new strains of Borders and Pinks, which it is hoped will be on the market in a year or so.

Picotee Borders

The cultivation of Picotees is identical to that of the Border carnations; perhaps they would be classed as a little hardier. Picotees are easily distinguished from their more conventional relatives as they are always either white or yellow, very delicately marked with a band of colour around the edge of each petal only.

Flakes and Bizarres

The Flake Border carnation is a combination of two or more distinct colours. The Bizarre Border carnation however is always of more than two colours, usually suffused one into the other. Again these carnations are cultivated in the same way as Border carnations and, like these, should never be 'stopped'. Both Bizarres and Flakes have gone out of favour, yet both are worthy of a place in any garden.

Pinks

Pinks are totally different from either Perpetual Flowering or Border carnations, however they are on a par with Borders as far as hardiness is concerned and are very easy to grow. They are often seen hiding in rockeries or growing in troughs. Their principal needs are an open well-drained position with full sunlight, and they should receive very little fertiliser if they are not to become too soft and bushy. These plants can be left to flower freely or disbudded for larger blooms. Pinks are not necessarily pink as the name suggests, but are named for their saw-toothed or picoted petal edges. They have a delightful range of colours, from pure white, pink and mauve to a wide range of two-toned ones. They are very popular in England, being suited to the climate. The varieties of pinks on display at the Chelsea Flower Show make one wonder why they are not used more in Australia in the cooler districts, for the size and quality of the flowers grown for showing in England would please any gardener.

Seed Carnations

No book on carnations would be complete without mention of the popular seed carnation. Seedlings are readily available at supermarkets and nurseries for those gardeners who do not wish to raise their own from seed.

Flowers will appear about 28 weeks after planting, so with seed carnations it is possible to control the time of flowering, if blooms are required for a special display. Sometimes councils use these to border rose gardens to good effect. Indeed, the wide range and variety of colours makes them worthy of a place in any garden. Though they have smaller blooms than the Perpetual Flowering varieties (see p. 41), the strong perfume and ease of growing make them quite an attractive proposition. They are often used to mix with less perfumed varieties in floral arrangements. Strains in seed packets are Gems of France, a mixture of French Chaubad Giants (fringed) and Fragrance (a bushy type), Enfants-de-France (plain-edged) and Chaubad Giants.

Unlike the named varieties which are propagated vegetatively, seed carnations are a matter of pot luck as far as colour goes. Keeping the seed from particular carnations will not guarantee the colour will be the same as the parent plant, but seed will be suitable for your next crop if required. Personally I would prefer to buy a packet of seed as they are disease free and tested for germination. Colours range from white through all shades of pink, reds and yellow, and occasionally two-toned ones.

Ensure that you obtain a top quality seed raising mix. Look for a soilless fine textured mixture that wets easily, is light, firm but airy and drains well yet retains the right amount of moisture for plant development. Alternatively you can make up your own using $1/2$ to $2/3$ sphagnum or peat moss with the remainder perlite or vermiculite or a combination of the two.

It is a good idea to sterilise (actually pasteurise) the mix to minimise the danger of damping off, or other harmful organisms. Fill a baking dish with moist mix, not wet; seal in an oven bag and place in the oven, set at 83°C or 180°F. Once the temperature has reached the right mark, leave for 30 minutes. Do not overheat. Do not plant until soil is absolutely cold.

Use a clean container at least 10 cm deep. Fill loosely with moist seed raising mix, then firm evenly with light pressure to around 2 cm from the top. Sow seed approximately 6 mm deep and firm down.

Water with disease preventing fungicide such as Benlate or Zineb. Cover with glass or put the tray in a polythene bag and close the end with a rubber band. At first sign of germination, usually 14-21 days at about 21°C, open bag to allow air to circulate, removing plastic bag or glass completely after two days. Keep shaded from direct sunlight and ensure the soil is kept moist but not wet. Most seed raising mixtures contain little or no nutrients, so as soon as small plants are visible, mist spray them with dilute liquid fertiliser at quarter strength. Repeat the fertilisation after each watering until seedlings are large enough to transplant.

Selecting Cultivars

There is now a wide variety of carnations available, but it has been rather hard to find them, with growers supplying only blocks of 50 plants of the one colour. When you do find a grower able to fill your requirements, it may be four to six weeks before they are ready, as they will be propagated after the order is taken.

Sims Perpetual Flowering varieties are often available through supermarkets, where they are sold in little plastic tubes, ready for planting out. An experiment was recently carried out in Europe where six packs of carnation, three fancies and three plain colours were trialled. The experiment was a success as these plants came from top quality stock, and were soon snapped up. It is hoped to start this type of selling in Australia in the near future. One agent in each state will have the franchise to market through supermarkets.

Special colours and some named varieties, especially the newest ones, will only be available from nurseries, as there is such a large range. The new carnation that catches your eye at the florist's may not be available to the average gardener. Some of these blooms will have a patent on them, and royalties must be paid by the grower to acquire the plant. A contract or agreement is drawn up, whereby the grower agrees not to propagate from that plant and to sell only the bloom from it.

If you are buying cultivars, or bringing them interstate, remember to make sure the firm you are dealing with has quarantine clearance for interstate buyers. If not, your plants, when you receive them will have every speck of soil washed away from the roots and be quite useless. Plants grown in soil may not be allowed through State borders; this definitely applies to Western Australia, so it would be wise to check it out first. Plants that are struck in a mixture of peat moss, perlite and polystyrene (the three Ps), a medium not conducive to disease, are acceptable for transporting interstate.

At one time, plants arrived in wet moss, sawdust and a piece of bag, and you were lucky to get 100 per cent out of your order. Now with modern rooting mixtures, 100 per cent is virtually guaranteed.

People often ask why you cannot get the complete range of colours from a packet of seeds. To get the true colour of the mother plant, it must be propagated vegetatively. Grow from your own cuttings or buy from a reputable grower. Seeds will come to bloom any colour, due to lack of control in the pollinating process. To get a new carnation, growers cross-pollinate by hand, carefully labelling the stock plant and the cross-pollinator. The seed collected is planted, then a seven or eight months wait is necessary to see if there is a plant of any quality. Many plants will be useless, producing only single blooms, ones with five or six petals, or a plant may be long and straggly and unable to produce a healthy shoot for further propagating. Three seasons of the cultivar growing to the true colour and type are necessary before it can be named and registered. This is a very time-consuming operation, for which very few people have the facilities, and it puts into perspective the cost of named carnations to the buyer.

There are many varieties in name and colour, and it can be very confusing to the average home gardener, especially when a bloom that appears to be the same as the one you have at home has a different name. The explanation is that two or three growers may perfect a new carnation, and register it, each giving it his choice of name, yet there may be very little noticeable difference in the colour. Also a plant may be subject to rust or wilt, and a new plant of the same colour will be perfected to replace it and a new name given.

Sims Perpetual Flowering carnation called 'Flamingo' is a real flamingo pink, yet the Avonmore 'Flamingo' is pink with yellow shadings.

Buy only sturdy healthy plants; do not bother with wilted or weak and lanky cultivars. There is no point in spending time and money on a plant that is not looking in top condition, when the reason for buying it in the first place is to upgrade your stock.

Two years is all you should keep a multi-coloured or two-toned carnation. I have found they revert back to the dominant colour after two years, while the cuttings taken in the first season remain the original colour until their third year. A carnation that is half white with a red stripe and half red is nothing more than a novelty.

I have a carnation, 'Andrea', that will throw a bloom on every plant with the white ground of the petals looking bloodshot. The heavy dark red blend seems to run like a dye through the white. The bloom is of perfect form, yet the shoots propagated from it grow true to the mother plant. I thought for a few years I had discovered a new carnation, but each plant only puts out two or three blooms of this strange colour. This is usually referred to as a renegade bloom and classified as a 'sport'.

Dianthus

Seed carnations and dianthus are regarded as annuals, but if the plants are cut back after the first flowering and given liquid fertiliser they will flower quite satisfactorily the second year.

Dianthus are the most adaptable of the carnation family as they tolerate a wider range of soils and will do well in rockeries or dry conditions. They are excellent border plants, producing large quantities of fragrant flowers in white, reds, mauves and pinks.

Varieties range from dwarfs 10 cm high to the 20 cm high variety useful for cut flowers.

The same conditions will suit all carnations, though the Perpetual Flowering varieties need a little more care than other types.

Seed carnations are easily renewed each year; with the other varieties it is advisable to take cuttings every year or second year to maintain a healthy supply. Some of my favourite colours have been with me for 22 years, because of the new cutting I take each year. It is a good policy to renew plants every two years. Although they will keep going many more years with cutting back, this is not really worth the time and effort as blooms get smaller as the plant ages. The main stem and roots will also start to deteriorate, often cracking and spitting, allowing the retention of water; this causes rotting and invites wilt and rust.

Classification of Colours

Bizarres have a clear ground marked and flaked with two or three colours—crimson, scarlet, pink or purple—and are categorised according to the predominant colour (crimson Bizarres, pink and purple Bizarres etc.).

Flakes have a clear ground flaked with one colour—scarlet, purple or rose (scarlet flakes, purple flakes etc.).

Selfs are of any one shade, the clearer and more definite the better.

Fancies are varieties not falling into any of the above classes, having a yellow or white ground or mottled, flaked or spotted with various colours.

Picotees have the colours confined to the margins of the petals.

Some years back a technique was used to dye carnations. This was a success with some commercial growers when introduced into Australia. It was used mostly for effect at weddings or Christmas, when a special colour was required. Systemic dying took 48 hours and only first-grade blooms could be used. Now colours are manipulated by tissue culture, and genetic engineering only. Chemicals have lost favour in horticultural experiments.

It is difficult to keep track of carnation names and varieties. One grower in Queensland may be tired of a particular red, for instance. He lets that plant lapse in favour of a different red, while the grower in South Australia may find the first red more popular. When a grower discontinues a variety, someone in another state may find it sells well. I found this personal preference normal with most growers, making it hard to be sure if a plant was still available.

I visited one farm in South Australia, where five hundred different varieties were on trial. Less than half will be suitable for reproduction. Many will have crooked or weak stems. The bloom may be imperfect, buds may split, colour may be uneven. The propagator is responsible for cultivating suitable carnations for general distribution.

Usually a plant takes three years to prove itself worthy of a name.

New colours of cyclamen, gold, green and deep burgundy are a few of the exciting new ones. The mixed colours are too many to contemplate. With so many lists of new species, no one has any idea how many there are.

One grower who supplies the florists in Canberra, grows only the Lulu variety. He had only three plain colours in them, but the perfect, uniform, smooth-edged blooms about 5 cm across are very popular with florists. The plant grows with a multitude of stems, rather than many buds per stem.

More plants are available from overseas every year and with Australian growers' breeding programs, lists need to be updated regularly. All these plants carry a patent are only available to registered flower growers, who pay a royalty to help cover the cost of further hybridisation. Many Standards and Sprays, all the Gipsy, Mini Micro and Chinesini fall into this category.

Since they are not available to the home gardener, they are dealt with separately later.

Hydroponics

Carnations respond very well to hydroponic culture. It is not something I have tried, but those who do try it, see good results.

All large nurseries have an automatic feeding system, whether they grow their carnations in the soil or on benches. Carnations grown in the soil need support, whereas carnations grown on benches are allowed to fall naturally.

The outer petals of carnations do not curl, when blooms are allowed to fall naturally. The plant stand described on page 28 also keeps the outer petals flat.

Cultivation

Soil Preparation

Any free-draining, well aerated soil from sand to sandy or gravelly loam is suitable for carnation growing. Soils must be open and light; sandy soil needs well rotted cow or horse manure. Pure sand needs a thorough lime dressing; a few weeks later add well decayed cow manure, bone dust and compost or leaf mould, then mix in thoroughly. Heavy soils need sand, crushed brick or vermiculite to aid drainage. Soil that is too heavy will not allow plants to develop properly and they will tend to be stunted with a slow yield of inferior flowers.

A strong dressing of lime is necessary on heavy soils, followed 3 weeks later with a good quality stable manure, bone dust, compost and sand. Sandy soils require about a handful of lime (generally about 100 gm) per square metre, heavy soils will probably require a bit more. If you have a soil tester handy, or can borrow a pH tester, it only takes a few minutes to check if the soil is suitably alkaline, with a pH of 6.8–7.5.

Carnations do not like their feet wet and need less water than other plants in the garden; they will mix in well with other plants, but do best on their own. Sandy soils help keep fungoid diseases in check.

Four or five days before planting, if soil has not been prepared as above, add a suitable fertiliser, rose fertiliser or Gro-plus, at a rate of approximately a third of a cup per square metre. I find a small yoghurt container useful as a measure, being about 1 cup.

Another suitable mix would be 4 parts potato manure E, 3 parts blood and bone, 1 part sulphate of potash. Dig in to only half the depth of the spade or fork. Wood ash added to any type of soil is beneficial to carnations. Potash is essential to their well being and can be used if preparing the ground with manures, but not if a complete fertiliser is used. Any of these ground preparations would provide sufficient nutrients to sustain plants to budding, when further feeding will be required to maintain large healthy blooms.

Bone dust enriches the soil; it has a slow effect but lasts longer than manures. Blood manure is very concentrated and a valuable fertiliser; it is quick in action. It may be scattered around plants and lightly forked in. If using it in a liquid form, mix 3 gm in 1 litre of water, and use as a liquid fertiliser just as buds form. If fowl manure is to be used, mix it with sawdust; fowl and sheep manures are too strong for carnations, making plants weak and grassy with few flowers. Nitrate of soda and sulphate of ammonia are the two most concentrated of the nitrogenous fertilisers and should only be used to stimulate young growth.

Slaked lime cannot be overestimated. It is necessary for growth and makes the soil sweeter, warmer and more porous, releasing food from manures and making it available to the roots of the plant. Lime added to clay soil lessens the adhesive properties and makes it friable when dry. Do not use lime directly before or after using manures containing ammonia, as lime neutralises the effect of it.

Soil should be properly prepared to give the best results. After planting, do not let the soil around the plants become compacted; soil needs to be aerated and a light raking or scarifying may be required. Carnations like crushed eggshells scratched in around them as they contain lime and help aerate the soil.

Situation

Carnations grow best in an open sunny position away from tall plants and fences. A fence may provide some protection from the weather, but the plants will lean outward towards the area where the light is brightest, leaving them straggly and weak.

Avoid afternoon shade as evening dampness encourages rust. A windy situation needs protection from the wind or the flowers will bruise or snap off. Above all do not plant where the ground does not completely dry out.

Planting

Never put a new plant into a hole in dry soil. Fill the hole with water two or three times, and moisten the filling soil you will use around the roots. Hold plants upright keeping the crown well above the surface. Fill in and firm a little at a time, making sure the crown is 3–4 cm above the soil surface. Carnations are not surface rooters and like a cool deep root run. The crown of the plant should be well above the soil surface, as any leaves in the soil will rot off and collar rot usually sets in.

Plants need to be spaced about 50 cm apart for gardeners who do not like work, and rows should be 75 cm apart. Narrow beds are more convenient for ease of working. My carnations grow successfully 20 cm apart, but require constant care. Commercial growers will grow them much closer, but they keep their plants for one season only. There is a high risk of infection in mass growing.

Do not plant in winter as cold checks the growth of the plants. The best time for rooted plants is from August to October or from March to April but not later, unless you are in an area of mild winters. Plants need some protection to flower successfully in cold weather, as rain, hail and strong winds bruise and snap off the buds. A plastic igloo to keep plants warm will keep the buds forming, or they can be kept in a glasshouse in pots and put out into the garden when the weather warms up. Take care not to keep them in a humid environment or rust will definitely take hold.

I grow my carnations in the garden all the year around but I have made frames covered with a strong clear plastic, about 1 metre high and the length of the flower bed. I place these on the three coldest sides of the flower bed. If there is an impending hail storm I might peg a large plastic bag over a couple of special plants, but generally they stand up well.

It is simple to make a wooden rake to mark out the spaces you wish to plant; this helps keep the rows and spaces uniform, and is also handy for marking out rows when planting vegetables. The one I use at present is spaced at 26 cm.

Carnations are not happy growing close to a fibro fence; they will grow there but never seem to have the quality of those grown elsewhere. Since the effect is not the same if they are grown near a picot fence, apart from the tendency to lean outwards, I suspect the problem is one of ventilation.

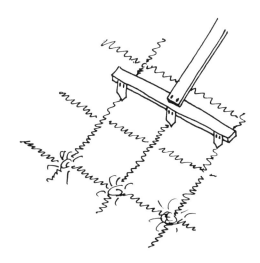

Watering

Watering depends a lot on the weather. Carnations do not like to be wet, if it is possible to keep plants dry when watering so much the better. Commercial growers use automatic trickle systems to avoid wetting the plants. For home gardeners it is advisable to water in the mornings as evening watering leaves the plant damp overnight and encourages stem rot.

The old adage of little and often is quite wrong for carnations. During the winter, little water is needed, but in the summer a constant watch should be kept to see the plants do not dry out. High afternoon summer temperatures may make the plants wilt, but do not take pity on them and give them a drink unless you can do so without wetting the leaves, as damp and humid conditions are a sure invitation for rust.

Carnation leaf should snap when bent over; if it folds like paper then it is too dry at the roots. I find a seaweed mulch very useful in the hot weather as it keeps the roots cool, stops drying out, contains some potash, is slightly alkaline and greatly benefits the plants. If I need to leave my garden over the holidays I always apply a good seaweed mulch. I have left the carnations for three weeks without water and never lost a plant. People with no access to seaweed should try alfalfa hay.

I watched one old gentleman test his beds with a piece of brass rod pointed at the end with about a third of its diameter cut away. He pushed it into the soil about 18 cm, if it came out clean he said it was watering time; soil sticking to the rod indicated it was damp enough. This works quite well for potted plants and saves water.

Staking

Staking is an important point to remember, as carnation plants do not like to be left lying on the ground and staking is necessary. Commercial growers use wire frameworks to keep the stems upright, increasing the height of the frame as the plants mature. Home gardeners can use any garden stakes or pieces of bamboo and tie up their plants. It is important to keep the plant upright at all times if you require a tall straight stem for your blooms.

I have a frame either end of the bed with cross pieces, and run garden twine between each row of plants, then tie cross pieces of twine across the beds between plants making a grid. It is the same as the wire system used by commercial growers, but it allows me to make the grid to suit the spacing of the plants. Pegs are put in at intervals to stop the twine sagging.

Solarisation

Many years ago a neighbour got sooty mould in his tomatoes. It soon became evident in my pumpkins, tomatoes and onions. In six months it started spreading to my carnations. It was so difficult to control, I burned most of my plants and kept the best in pots in the glasshouse. I did not plant in that ground for four years, letting the chooks run on it.

Some years later I was given a pamphlet on solarisation, based on tests being carried out by the University of California. I have been using a simple form of the idea for some years now with pleasing results.

Solarisation is the process of cleaning the soil using the heat of the sun's rays through plastic sheeting. Fungus diseases are arrested, nematodes disappear and the carnations thrive on the sterilised soil. The process also helps keep weeds down and there are fewer weed seeds to germinate.

You will need a sheet of clear plastic 0.1 mm thick, the size of the bed to be sterilised; a little larger is no problem since the edges are buried in soil as an anchor.

Cultivate the soil to a fine tilth and shape the bed to the size to be used later. Remove any clods or stones which make the surface uneven. Water well and then cover with the plastic sheet.

Dig a shallow trench at one end to bury the plastic and anchor it. Pull the rest of the plastic over the bed smoothly, and anchor the sides with soil. Pull tight and ease out any air pockets; the plastic should cling to the earth and air pockets will make it ineffective. Anchor the end with soil.

Leave in place for 4 weeks if the temperature is around 25°C, or until the bed is required. And of course don't walk on it, it holes the plastic.

I leave mine for up to 12 weeks over the winter months to reduce the weeds, take the plastic off, rake over a couple of times and plant in a few days. Planting can be done immediately; I just like to leave a couple of days to disturb any weeds that may germinate.

Feeding

From the time carnations are set out in the open there is no cessation of growth. They will bloom over a longer period than almost any other flower, Perpetual Flowering carnations retaining their usefulness, under congenial conditions, for 2-3 years without needing to be disturbed. These plants may be treated as annuals if desired, or they may be cut back to within 10 cm of the centre stem, side stems possibly needing to be shorter, to encourage fresh new growth. Flowers on two-year-old plants will be slightly smaller than in the first season, for as the plant gets older the blooms become smaller.

In winter plants will not grow much unless under shelter, and should not be fertilised to hurry up the growing period, which will occur naturally when the weather warms up. In spring and as warmer weather approaches new growth will be obvious. This is the time to give a light spring feed of liquid fertiliser. Feeding is then required at three week intervals until buds appear, and in summer weekly to keep the blooms coming along at an acceptable size.

I use Aquasol for a liquid feed but I change to Phostrogen when the buds are full; I also occasionally use fish emulsion. The plants seem to like the change and the blooms are larger without forcing the plant. Use all fertilisers as the producer recommends. My choice is purely personal preference; Thrive or any other liquid fertiliser is suitable when flowering stems appear, usually from September to March.

A good substitute for commercial liquid fertilisers is soot water as it improves the size and colour of blooms. I use 2 small yoghurt containers of soot to an 18 litre bucket of water, allow to stand 4 or 5 days and then feed plants. Take care not to get this in the blooms as a black mark will appear that needs washing off. I sometimes add a small yoghurt container of blood manure or 2 containers of blood and bone. This makes an excellent liquid fertiliser, but is a bit messy, so I give the plants a fine light spray with the hose to wash off any black.

I once grew carnations in a bed that had been fertilised with sheep manure the year before to grow lettuce. The carnations grew well enough but a higher than usual number of flowers split. The plants were also too green in colour and tended to grassiness with weak stems from too much nitrogen.

I tried Nitraphoska (blue) fertiliser on a carnation bed: the plants grew fast but were bright green and sappy looking. They were not the lighter dull green they should be, and leaves and stems were not crisp and brittle, as expected on a correctly controlled carnation.

Do not overfeed in the hope of obtaining more flowers, for you will find you have bigger plants with more foliage and fewer flowers, not the ultimate aim. These plants will not have that sharp silvery green look familiar to carnation growers everywhere, but will be sickly looking with buds that may hang limp from weak stems. This indicates they have been forced and need to dry out for a time. Do not feed again for 8–10 weeks and reduce watering to a minimum.

When beds reserved exclusively for carnations are not giving good results, a light dressing of common salt may be found to rejuvenate plants which do not respond to applications of the usual fertilisers; assuming of course that you have not overfertilised. This is not to be used where other plants are to be grown, although beetroot will also respond to this treatment.

I expect this is the reason carnations like a seaweed mulch, as I do not wash it before using on the garden. I collect the fine black seaweed as it rots down after two years, but the dry ribbon-like seaweed does not. A friend of mine used to collect this type and burn it in the garden; he had a fine vegetable plot.

Stopping

Translated this means pulling out the top two or three sets of leaves to literally stop the plant. This procedure makes the plant branch out at the stopped point and prevents long straggly unruly growth.

Once carnation plants reach a height of 10 to 14 cm they can be 'stopped'. This is done by pinching out the centre top leaves, so the plant will branch out at this point. When these new shoots are long enough, they also are stopped. This is necessary to make a compact plant with ten to twelve shoots which produce flowers when they grow taller.

Leaving only one or two shoots will produce a long straggly plant with only one flower. Once this bloom is taken, there will be no healthy 'breaks' from which new shoots will grow. Shoots that do grow will be weak and useless for propagating.

Whether you stop your plants before or after planting out is a matter for the individual grower. Do not do it while transplanting as it may contribute to disturbing the roots; give them two or three weeks to recover.

Some plants may not need to be stopped: Border carnations are already bushy, naturally, and have three or four small shoots before transplanting, while the Perpetual Flowering varieties will have one.

Do not drop the shoots or buds taken out in the garden. Place them in a bin for disposal as carnations particularly like a clean bed to grow in.

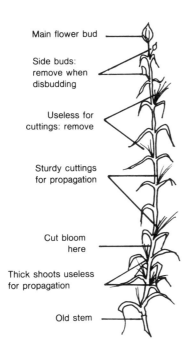

Main flower bud

Side buds: remove when disbudding

Useless for cuttings: remove

Sturdy cuttings for propagation

Cut bloom here

Thick shoots useless for propagation

Old stem

Stop here

Allow 6 months from the time the plant is stopped for it to flower. Stopping shoots selectively each week allows the plant to flower over an extended period, which is not the case if all stopping is done at the same time.

First stop

Plant ready for second stopping

Disbudding

With the warmer weather your carnations will send out many buds per stem: disbudding is the grower's choice. Perpetual Flowering carnations should be disbudded regularly with the aim of producing larger blooms of good quality. To achieve this it is necessary to remove unwanted side buds as soon as this can be done without damage to the main bud or bruising the plant stem. The flower will not be bigger unless disbudding is done early.

To remove unwanted side buds and growth further down the plant, pull sideways and downwards and they should snap off easily. Do not drop on the ground but place in a bin for disposal.

Take care with the top bud and note its angle to the stem. Occasionally a top bud will be damaged and shoot out sideways, so that the flower hangs at an unsightly angle or snaps off. It would be better to remove this bud and allow the next best bud to develop.

Disbudding differs with each class of carnation as some are short-stemmed varieties and it is personal choice whether you want one, two or three flower buds per stem. The more buds per stem the smaller the flower. Perpetual Flowering carnations are tall growers and the bottom buds can develop after the top bud has been harvested.

While disbudding, remove unwanted shoots that appear between the top sets of leaves. The top ones are long and spindly and too weak for propagation; discard these and choose from shoots that are second or third down the stem. Shoots and buds that are discarded could have tiny specks of rust; dropping these on the ground encourages more to develop.

Carnations can be planted at any time of the year, however it is prudent to time your cuttings to when blooms are required. Mid summer and mid winter are not the best time to keep shoots for propagating; although they will grow, the plants will stagnate in winter.

Calyx Splitting

Well formed calyces are imperative for producing good blooms. The calyx should be bell shaped, with sufficient brackets to support the petals and allow for expansion.

Split calyx can be inherited, another reason to be particular when taking shoots for rooting. Little can be done with a carnation plant with a poorly formed calyx.

Sudden differences in temperature will also add to this problem. Cool weather slows down the flowering process, or retards the opening of the petals. The flower continues to grow, making more petals, and the calyx is not large enough to accommodate them, causing it to burst. This is most prevalent in spring and autumn. Splitting does not occur until some weeks after the drop in temperature, therefore it is advisable to watch for sudden fluctuating weather conditions. If the flower is for a special occasion, protection from the weather will help.

Incorrect feeding and a high imbalance of nitrogen and potassium adds to the problem, yet split calyx still occurs in correctly fertilised carnation beds.

Good breeding of the new carnations has almost defeated calyx splitting; very few of the ones bred in the last four years suffer this problem. A rubber band slipped over a bud showing signs of splitting should help. Ties from freezer bags will also suffice as a temporary measure.

To protect a special bud from damage, the following method is especially useful when preparing a bloom for showing:

Drill a 2 cm hole in the centre of a flat board, cut a ½ cm slit in to the centre and nail board to a garden stake. Place firmly in the ground beside the carnation bud, slide the bud that is showing colour into the centre hole. Now place a 12–14 cm earthenware flower pot on the board thus protecting the bloom until it opens perfectly.

Once a bloom has a split calyx it loses its appeal and looks untidy when displayed with perfect specimens in a floral arrangement. To repair the split, gently press the petals back into place, hold the calyx together until the split closes up, then with a No 8 rubber band spread between thumb and two fingers, ease up the stem onto the split calyx.

Specialists in floriculture now have a new calyx clip which clips into the split calyx to repair it and is extremely effective as its shape and colour merge into the form of the plant. These may also be available from commercial carnation growers.

Nevertheless a split calyx detracts from the beauty of the bloom, and a carnation with a split calyx can never be accepted for display at a show, even with the new clips. Correct fertilising and general care can reduce the problem.

Split calyx

Propagation

The importance of propagating only from first class, disease free stock cannot be overstressed. You are going to get a replica of the mother plant, so do not waste time and space on something that is not top quality.

Cuttings

Cuttings are taken from a flowering stem. Each stem will produce about ten pairs of leaves, from which grow the side shoots, either discarded at the time disbudding is being done, or kept for propagating.

The top two shoots are of no use, as they will produce a long spindly plant with no substance and poor flowers. Generally these shoots have leaves too far apart.

The second and third shoots produce the best plant, and will bloom the same as the mother plant. Leaves on these shoots will be firmer and situated closer together.

The bottom shoots are thick and stubby and, if grown, will result in a fine bushy green plant but very few flowers.

Sims and Avonmore carnations, being tall and vigorous growers, will produce sufficient side shoots to choose from, while the shorter or Border carnations are sometimes better layered.

It is a mistake to sneak a shoot off old Aunt Mary's favourite carnation plant. It could be a poor quality plant or prone to disease. Unless you see the bloom is of top quality, and the shoot itself is the right one for reproducing quality flowers, then don't waste your time.

Remember diseases of the mother plant will come out in the propagated cutting. If you are doing a lot of cuttings at the same time, it is wise practice to dip them in a mixture of fungicide and insecticide. Just dip the cuttings enough to wet them, then plant in a suitable rooting medium. Please wear gloves while working with chemicals; insecticides are very nasty when absorbed through the skin.

Cuttings should not be stood in water before planting. If there is some delay between taking the cutting and planting, wrap the shoot in wet paper to prevent it drying out.

Take a cutting with the 'heel' intact by pulling downwards and away from the plant. With a razor blade cut just below the lower leaf node or joint. The next two leaves are removed and the cutting is ready to dip in rooting hormone, if desired, before planting. If it is possible to make a clean break at the lower node this is better, unless implements are dipped in a fungicide solution to avoid the possibility of spreading disease.

I am very particular about the cuttings I use, as I prefer not to use fungicides and insecticides where I may be in close contact with them. Usually my cuttings go straight into the boxes where they are to grow.

Select shoots about 7 to 10 cm long and, after trimming the base of the shoot, make a hole in the rooting medium with a pencil so as not to bruise the fibre of the shoot, plant it in the hole and gently press firm.

A mixture of equal parts of sand, perlite and granulated peat provides good aeration and drainage for cuttings. Sand is suitable if it does not dry out. Heavy soil is to be avoided as good drainage and aeration are important to get roots started. Richgo seed raising mixture is an excellent medium for raising cuttings.

Rooting hormones are readily available on the market and do get cuttings started quicker. Remember to get a hormone for softwood cuttings.

In warm and humid weather carnations will root in about three weeks, but will take longer in cooler months, unless they are under glass or plastic. In hotter months, cuttings need to be protected from hot drying winds, and kept moist and lightly shaded.

Some cuttings will be quicker to root than others, especially the more vigorous growers. Try not to take cuttings from plants dry at the roots as they are very slow to take. In cold conditions the cuttings will stagnate and be dormant until conditions are more suitable, or they may rot in the ground.

Synthetic rooting mixtures and sand provide no food for the cuttings, so when they show signs of growing after six or eight weeks give a light spraying of half strength Aquasol or Thrive or similar liquid fertiliser.

Often a cutting planted immediately below the mother plant will take faster than one given all the care in the world; this is nearly always so if planting a cutting from a fuchsia.

I have planted cuttings in a glasshouse, in seed boxes in a warm corner away from cold winds and in a garden bed. These were all done on the same day, using the same propagating mixture for the first two.

The cuttings in the seed box were the first to start growing. The cuttings in the garden were next and were stronger plants, while the cuttings in the glass house were two weeks later in the rooting process. This was in spring and I can only put it down to the evening dew on the cuttings keeping them crisp and fresh enough to avoid wilting.

A greater number of cuttings died or rotted off at ground level in the glasshouse than in either of the other situations. No situation was 100 per cent successful. The ideal conditions for cuttings are two hours of morning sun then shade or light shade. Hot sun on cuttings will dry them out, though winter sun is tolerable.

Once again the important thing to remember is that the cutting is only as good as the mother plant. A cutting from an inferior plant will never give a good bloom when full grown. It is definitely worth while to be selective. Time your cuttings so rooted plants are not being planted out in the middle of winter; cold checks the growth of the plant.

The best time for rooted plants is from August to October or March to April, but not later unless they are to be grown with some protection from the cold. Plants will flower in winter but rain and strong winds damage them and bruise the buds.

A plastic igloo to keep cultivars warm in winter will keep buds forming and flowering satisfactorily, and they can also be kept potted in the glasshouse and put out in the garden as soon as the weather warms up, even if in bud. However, carnations kept in a glasshouse or plastic igloo will not have the perfume of those grown out in the open and good ventilation is a necessity to get the full potential of the carnation bloom.

Cuttings taken in midsummer will flower in winter and those taken in winter, if grown under glass or plastic, will flower in midsummer.

Be sure your young plants have really taken root before you transplant them. Care must be taken not to damage the fine roots, or the plants will be retarded and possibly die.

The surest and best method of getting good stock is to buy from a suitable grower as plants will be strong and free of disease.

All of my carnations, whether in pots or the garden, get occasional side dressings of crushed eggshells scratched into the soil and soot, usually made up into liquid fertiliser. I keep the eggshells until there is a reasonable amount to crush; they contain lime, are light and help aerate the soil. Soot has always been one of the favourite fertilisers of the old Chinese gardeners, and they certainly knew how to grow things.

Layering

Layering carnations is an easier way of continuing supplies of good stock. Border carnations are relatively easy to layer; the taller varieties are more difficult unless the plant has gone straggly, leaving branches close to the ground.

The best time for layering would be soon after the earliest flowers are past their best, probably January–February, but it is worth trying any time a good low shoot is in the right place, on the right plant.

Again the quality of the young plant is only as good as the mother plant; select the strongest basal shoots from the best plant.

Make sure there is no lime or fertiliser near the shoot being layered.

The medium for layering should be a light sandy one with some compost, peat or leaf mould; here I use a little fine seaweed in the mixture. Choice of layering mixtures can be as for rooting cuttings. Mix lightly into the topsoil around the plant.

Choose a layer with about 8 to 10 sets of leaves; remove the bottom ones, leaving six top leaves. With a sharp knife slice halfway through the stem, at least one node

31

below the lower leaves on the shoot. Make a sliced cut leaving a 'tongue'. The shoot to be layered is still joined to the main plant on the top side and care must be taken not to snap it off.

Bend the 'tongue' down into the rooting mixture, gently holding the shoot in a slightly upright position. Press firmly around the plant, and secure with a pin or bent piece of wire; a fern or bracken frond also does the job of keeping it in position until rooted. When the layers are set, water in with a fine spray to ensure the mixture does not dry out. Further watering will depend on weather conditions.

It will take about 5 weeks for the layer to be rooted; this is the time to separate the two by cutting the connection, without disturbing the layer. Leave it undisturbed for 3 days or 3 weeks until you are ready to transplant it to its final growing spot.

Potted plants can be layered in the same way by standing small pots of rooting mixture around the mother plant. Special care must be taken here as small pots dry out quickly, yet keeping them wet will cause rot.

An instructive experiment which I carried out was where I took a shoot from a stalk that had an imperfect flower; the petals were small and curled up, the flower slightly split. The rest of the plant had perfect flowers, but I wished to experiment with the shoot from an inferior bloom.

The first year the flowers from that shoot were all small and curled up at the edges. The following year it produced one flower that was of acceptable quality. I took a shoot from that stalk and grew it. The resulting flowers were small and inferior, petals uneven and curled up, occasionally a split calyx, but it produced two good flowers. I kept up this procedure to see if it was possible to grow a good quantity of quality flowers from a shoot originally on a poor quality flower stem. After six seasons of failure, I discarded all the plants, and will stress the point to anyone. Quality stock is an absolute necessity for getting quality blooms.

1. 'Amethyst' (p. 60)

2. 'Duberry' (p.60)

3. 'Jon Cleary' (p. 63)

4. 'Laika' (p. 61)

5. 'Lavender Lace' (p. 61)

6. 'Pink Ice' (p. 62)

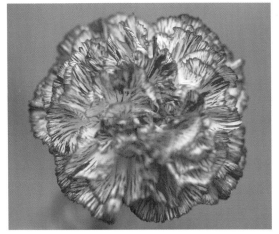

7. 'Red Diamond' (p.62)

8. 'Red Diamond' at 3 years (p. 62)

9. 'Red Diamond' at 4 years (p. 62)

10. 'Storm' (p. 62)

11. 'Tangerine' (p.62)

12. 'Telstar' (p. 62)

13. 'Tigre' (p. 62)

14. 'Zamora' (p. 63)

15. 'Aravelo' (p. 60)

16. 'Candy' (p. 60)

17. 'Fiona' (p. 60)

18. 'Flamingo' (p. 60)

19. 'Lolita' (p. 61)

20. 'Lyndal' (p. 61)

21.'Madeline' (p. 61)

22. 'Opal' (p.61)

23. 'Orchard Beauty' (p. 61)

24. 'Rosette' (p. 62)

25. 'Safari' (p. 62)

26. 'Sally' (p. 62)

27. ' Dark Pierrot' (p. 60)

28. 'Delphi' (p. 60)

29. 'Dona' (p. 60)

30. *Left clockwise* 'Echo', 'Roland', 'Unesco' (p. 65)

31. *Left* 'Exquisite', *Right* 'Brio' (p. 64)

32. 'Gala' (p. 60)

33. 'Izerali' (p. 61)

34. 'Izmir' (p. 61)

35. 'Kiwi Gem' (p. 63)

36. 'Kristina' (p. 61)

37. 'Las Palmas' (p. 61)

38. 'Laurella' (p. 61)

39. 'Liberty' (p. 61)

40. 'Lisboa' (p. 61)

41. 'Malaga' (p. 61)

42. 'Master' (p. 61)

43. ' Mei Bao' (p. 65)

44. 'Mei Fu' (p. 65)

45. ' Nelson' (p. 61)

46. 'Orange Magic' (p. 61)

47. 'Prado' (p. 62)

48. 'Prissi Anne' (p. 63)

49. 'Purple Rendevous' (p. 62)

50. 'Raggio de Sole' (p. 62)

New strains of carnation developed over the last ten years, have made a wide range to choose from, with much variation in the size of the blooms.

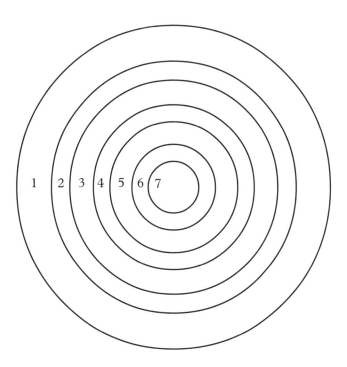

Ring	1	Standard
	2	Border
	3	New Spray Range
	4	Pinks, Fields
	5	Micro
	6	Mini Micro
	7	Gipsy

Pests and diseases

The most common enemies of carnations are aphids, red spider or spider mite, thrip and native bud worm. There are also snails, slugs, earwigs, wireworms and caterpillars. Diseases most common are rust, leaf spot and wilt. This sounds like a formidable array of problems but a well looked after, clean garden rarely has much to worry about.

Aphids

More than one hundred different species of aphids have been recorded in Australia. They come in various colours, green, black, pink and even bright yellow, and most are between 1.5 and 2 mm long, that is a little bigger than a pin head. These tiny monsters are sap sucking and cause serious damage, especially as they increase rapidly when food is plentiful and the weather warm. Aphids can first be seen on the underside of the leaves, sucking out the life, causing discolouration, distortion and wilting.

They reproduce about every 7 days, and carry virus diseases, so watch out for them as soon as the warm weather arrives.

To control, regularly inspect plants for aphids, and other beneficial insects. Birds, spiders, lacewings, predatory bugs and beetles, parasitic flies and wasps attack aphids. Spraying with chemicals also destroys these insects. Chemicals to use if necessary are systemic sprays such as Rogor, Lebaycid or Malathion.

Thrip

Thrip are often not noticed until considerable damage has been done because they are inconspicuous, feeding out of sight on the underside of leaves and flowers. Their mouthparts are said to be rasping and they feed by damaging the surface of the plant and sucking the sap out; leaves become a dull silver or grey. They attack an unopened bud leaving irregular white marks on the bloom. When stem and leaves are attacked the crushed surface will heal with a brown scab.

Survival of hibernating thrip is promoted by above average rainfall in autumn, a mild winter, a sunny spring and plenty of host flowers, like capeweed. Thrip life cycle is 10 days to a month, depending on temperature. Spray as for aphids.

Red Spider

Red spider is not really a spider but a tiny mite about 1 mm in length. They puncture the tissue of the foliage and suck out the cell content. These tiny punctures cause minute white scars on the leaves, which lose their blue-green healthy appearance and become dull grey. The plant may become weakened and will die if this pest is not controlled.

The life cycle of mites can be up to 4 weeks depending on weather temperature. Spray the same as for aphids, again in 7 days, then again in 14 days, as all stages of mite will be found at the same time.

Even when the adult mite is killed, eggs will hatch in six days when the temperature is about 16°C and over. As this pest breeds well in lawns, spraying the surrounding area of the garden is necessary. In spring, spraying at intervals of six days is necessary until pests are controlled.

Caterpillars

Caterpillars damage carnation buds, eating the bud from the inside, and are unobserved until empty buds occur. The culprit is detected when you open the hollow bud.

Whitefly

Whitefly will attack carnations if they are feeding on other garden plants but I have not had whitefly in my carnations as the bed is isolated. I have had whitefly on a lantana bush and I used the old remedy of the yellow board.

A yellow board is painted with any sort of oil, and the fly shaken off onto the board; the fly sticks in the oil and dies. It appears that whitefly is attracted to the bright colour of the yellow.

Snails and Slugs

Slugs and snails love carnation beds; they get in the cool areas under leaves and around the base of the plant and are a menace to the flowers, leaving them with bits chewed out of the petals.

These pests will avoid crawling through borders of sawdust, ashes or lime sand. They do like a bit of beer and a saucer of beer left out overnight will attract snails, who then drown themselves.

The Organic Growers Association recommends taking two to three inches of rope, saturating it with sump oil and leaving it where snails gather. It doesn't say whether the snails eat the rope or hang themselves.

I pick the snails off early in the morning and give them to the chooks. One book suggests the snails you handpick can be served at that evening's dinner. They are a good source of nourishment, offering 12 to 16 per cent protein and just 100 calories in 100 grams of meat.

Native bud worm moth

Grubs destroy blooms

Native Bud Worm

Native bud worms are tiny grubs which hatch in the bud and destroy the petals. Tiny holes in the bud may be the only indication they have arrived; then you find buds drying up unopened. The eggs are laid by a small mottled brown moth the size of a 5-cent piece. Usually this pest is most prevalent in hot weather, mid summer to autumn.

A systemic spray is needed to combat this pest. As the worm has to eat the flower before dying, the bloom will be ruined anyway.

For native bud worm and other caterpillars, spray with systemic spray, then again in 7 days and again in 3 weeks. This generally gets rid of them until next year.

Western Flower Thrip

Western flower thrip is a relatively new pest in Australia. It is similar in appearance and biology to the common thrip. Due to its efficiency in spreading tomato spotted wilt virus, it has cost growers millions of dollars in Asia, Canada, Europe, New Zealand and the U.S.A.

It was discovered in Western Australia in 1993 and has since spread to New South Wales and Queensland.

Western flower thrip feed and reproduce on a wide range of plants, from vegetables, ornamental plants, fruit, cut flowers, strawberries, peanuts and tobacco. It can consume 12.5% of its body weight per hour. In addition to the damage it causes, it can spread various wilt diseases. This pest is hunted by all Agricultural and Quarantine Departments in all States.

You may have this pest if (a) there is a larger thrip population than usual, (b) they are difficult to control or (c) they are on a wide range of plants.

To trap thrip, shake infested leaves over thick white paper, then tip any dislodged thrip into a jar of methylated spirits. The Agricultural Department will identify them for you. Blue or white boards painted with oil or other sticky substance, and placed under plants will attract thrip.

Soil Pests

Wireworms, eelworms, nematodes and earwigs can be destroyed by sterilising the soil. Commercial growers sterilise their soil regularly, but it is not so easy for the home gardener.

I solarise my carnation beds and change them every two years; most of my carnations are grown in the vegetable garden area, where crop rotation is practised.

There are suitable chemicals on the market such as Thimet that will control soil pests, but they also kill the worms, and are not suitable where food crops are grown.

Rust

Rust has been known to infest carnations as long as they have been cultivated. Although it can ruin a plant, it can be controlled. It is a fungus disease caused by humid conditions and overwatering; its incidence can be lessened by avoiding these situations.

Rust looks like dark brown blisters, and can spread rapidly if moisture is left on plants late in the day. Humidity and dampness are its breeding ground; plenty of ventilation is required to allow the plants to dry after watering.

Incorrect feeding or the use of unbalanced fertilisers, especially if they induce fast soft growth, will encourage rust. Too much nitrogen will quickly make carnations soft and sappy with no resistance to rust.

Spores are spread from plant to plant by wind and water splash. Leaf wetness is necessary for infection. The disease is common under warm humid conditions. Avoid wet foliage and overhead watering.

Rust is easily spread by cutting implements, secateurs, scissors or knife, unless sterilised before using on the next plant. Sterilisation can be achieved by dipping secateurs in boiling water or a suitable fungicide. I prefer to break or snap carnations to avoid infection. Any infected leaves or branches are taken off and burned.

Commercial growers use Baycor 300 for rust but at $130 per litre undiluted, it is not a good investment for a few garden plants. It is now available in spray cans. Fine ash sprinkled on the plants will deter rust. Sprays to use include Mancozeb, Zineb and Benlate.

Leaf Spot

Leaf spot is a circular or slightly oblong spot on the leaves with a brownish centre and a darker ring around it. It is caused by similar conditions to rust, and cold damp nights. Carnations in pots or where they are protected from evening moisture are less likely to get leaf spot.

Mildew

Mildew is a fine white powdery fungus occurring in late summer and affecting both buds and leaves. It is usually caused by dry root conditions. As with all fungus diseases, once it gets a hold it will spread quickly. Karathane dust is effective, but if the plants are at the end of their season, it would be wiser to burn them and be rid of the problem.

Stem Rot

Stem rot and wilts are probably the most feared of all the diseases, especially by commercial growers, for once they start, they can wipe out the entire crop. Stem rot is caused by a fungus which inhabits the soil. It is sometimes referred to as damping off.

It attacks the plant at ground level, usually when the base of the plant has been damaged. Affected plants will start wilting and branches or the whole plant will disintegrate at ground level and come away from the roots. Brown knots of fungus may be seen at the rotted part of the stem This same fungus may attack cuttings being propagated.

BacterialWilt.

This is not caused by a fungus, but by bacteria entering the plant through the roots. The stem rots at soil level and the plant wilts rapidly. If the bark of the stem is removed, a yellow or brown discolouration may extend up into the branches. The stem will feel sticky and slimy at ground level. A clean garden is necessary to avoid this problem. It is something I have not seen for myself, thank goodness.

Wilts are most prevalent in wet hot weather. There is no chemical for the control of this disease.

Fusarium Wilt

This disease begins with the wilting of a single branch. The leaves become a dull green, then wilt and rapidly die. When the branch is cut lengthwise, the tissue directly under the bark will be yellow or reddish brown along the sap channels. It is better to take out the whole plant and burn it, than to hope some of it will recover. Eventually the whole plant will die as infection is through the roots.

Do not take a cutting from this plant. It is the most difficult disease to control, and even cuttings from the plants next to it should be avoided. The disease should not be a problem as long as clean and hygienic conditions have been maintained. Deep planting in the garden or pots should always be avoided. Do not plant another carnation in the same spot; the disease is in that piece of ground and another plant will most likely suffer the same fate.

Pest Control

Before I start on commercial means of pest control, I must point out my reluctance to use chemical sprays. A clean and healthy garden gives the best results and is safer and cheaper. Pests usually attack a plant that is already weak from poor conditions.

Some years ago I was tying up some tomato plants and, as I was using both hands to pull the branches up, I put the plastic garden tie in my mouth to hold. I immediately tasted Metasystox. Dropping everything I ran and washed my mouth out with the hose. I then washed my mouth out with soap and water from the bathroom. I have no idea how the chemical came to be on the garden tie.

I went back to finish my work. In one hour I was nauseous and dizzy, in three hours I was too ill to stand up or hold my head up, after ten hours in bed the symptoms were starting to dissipate. It was three days before I was well.

I have never had Metasystox in my shed again.

At some time every garden will be attacked by pests of some sort. Unfortunately plant damage caused by diseases and pests can be quickly controlled by chemical sprays, while the naturally-made sprays are often a little slower to work. All pesticides are toxic in some way, and should only be handled as the manufacturer advises. Doubling the amount recommended will not be beneficial or get quicker results.

If you are not sure of the correct pesticide, check with the Agriculture Department for the safest and most effective spray to use. Often it is advisable to take the pest to the department to be identified.

Wear rubber gloves and protective clothing and a hat; absorption through the skin is the least obvious means of contamination when sprays are being used. Should you accidentally splash yourself with pesticide wash it off immediately.

My carnations are grown near my vegetables and considerable care is taken when spraying for pests, and the withholding period for edible crops noted.

I am also unenthusiastic about Mesurol for snails. It has a withholding period of 42 days, which is a long time, and it makes me wonder if there is any residual effect. My snails are picked off the garden early in the morning and given to the chooks; of course I do not get them all, but it's a safe method.

Aphids can be controlled as for thrip or sprayed with pyrethrum or nicotine sulphate.

Red spider can be controlled with the systemic sprays and Malathion; I usually combine the two as Malathion is instant and systemic sprays last 14 days. I usually give one more spray after 10 days.

The Organic Growers Association claim their garlic spray has a mortality rate of 87 per cent for wireworms, 73 per cent for snails, 92 per cent for aphids and 98 per cent for white butterfly caterpillars.

The recipe: soak three ounces of chopped garlic in two teaspoons of mineral or liquid paraffin for 48 hours. Then add one pint of water and one ounce of pure soap. Store in a plastic container. Try different solutions at around one part of the mixture to 100 parts water.

A favourite plant of mine got rust. I cut it back to healthy shoots, removed all leaves with the slightest bit of rust, and as it grew I repeated the process. When the plant was free of the disease, I then used shoots for propagating new plants.

Rust, wilt and mildew are all treated much the same. All are difficult to control but can be kept down to a minimum by spraying in spring with a fungicidal spray. Zineb, Captan, Benlate, Dithane 45, and PlantVax are all effective. I never use the same spray two seasons running as resistance to a spray can lessen its effect. When spraying for these diseases I always add a systemic spray to discourage any leaf-eating pests.

Native bud worms will only be controlled by systemic sprays, so I use Rogor or Lebaycid; Dipel and Bugmaster 80 are also effective. As this little pest appears in late summer, the spray is mixed with a fungicide to reduce the chance of rust.

Slugs and snails of course investigate everyone's garden; slugs love sneaking into carnation buds and when the flower opens half the petals fall out. They inhabit any place damp and cool. Cabbage or rhubarb leaves spread on the ground will encourage them to crawl underneath, if there is no other suitable hiding spot. Sprinkling slugs with salt causes irritations that make them produce great quantities of slime, and they destroy themselves through dessication.

There are suitable products on the market to annihilate these pests: Baysol, Defender, Mesurol or metaldehyde which can be mixed with bran.

Wormwood tea sprayed on the ground will deter slugs and snails; it will also kill aphids.

Slaters will crawl into a hollowed out potato and are easily disposed of. Generally they are not a problem in a carnation bed, but will attack any plant growing along a fence, where they can crawl into cracks and breed. Chooks love them. They are difficult to control with sprays, because of their hiding places, but the insect spray Pea Beau will make them keel over quicker than anything else.

Agricultural Departments

Your local Agricultural Department puts out information on all sorts of pests and growing procedures and this is available to the public on request. While it is geared more to the commercial grower and farmer, it is useful to home gardeners as well.

If you are doubtful about a type of bug or disease infesting your garden, this is the place to go for the correct solution. The Agricultural Department also likes to keep track of any new outbreak of pests or disease.

My area had an invasion of army worms two years ago and it was the local Agricultural Department which came to the rescue with the correct solution.

However, the pamphlet put out by the Department on carnations is for the commercial grower. The fertiliser requirements are in such large quantities, it is not worth the hassle of breaking it down into small amounts.

While on the subject of purchasing fertiliser, when I tried to buy ammonium nitrate, I was given the big run-around. It took quite a while before someone told me a licence is required to purchase it.

Farmers use it for clearing stumps in paddocks. I would have been happier if told this in the first place. I have no intention of blowing up my garden shed or garage, where I sometimes keep my fertilisers.

Pots

Carnations can be successfully grown in pots on window ledges, verandahs or any area where they get a reasonable amount of sun. Remember sunshine and good ventilation are indispensible requirements for disease free carnations.

I grow quite a few carnations in pots. The ones I particularly like, especially if they have a good perfume, I bring inside at flowering time. When the flowers are finished, I take them out and plant them in the garden, after I have trimmed them back. I have found a carnation grown in the garden will always produce a better bloom than one grown in a pot.

Carnations can be made to bloom more freely, in any particular season, by cutting them back in the preceding season. If required in spring, cut them back in winter; if it is in autumn you want the blooms then cut them back in summer. This will induce better quality flowers than if they are left to bloom haphazardly. This applies to the Perpetual Flowering varieties only. Some of the others will react to this treatment, but not all, as some flower only in spring or autumn.

Take care in potting out the new seedlings. If they are bought, they were probably started in lightly shaded areas and putting them into direct sunlight or under glass could burn them. Start them off in diffused sunlight. Generally carnations grown in pots are started in tubes 5 or 6 cm wide, and gradually repotted two or three times until they are finally in 15 to 20 cm pots. At 8 cm pots a mixture of 3 parts loam 1 part old manure and 1 part garden ashes is recommended.

Soil mixture for any pots need to be well aerated, otherwise it clogs up, and carnations get stem rot.

I use a bushel box measuring 56 cm by 25 cm by 25 cm high for measuring my potting mixes in. It is equal to 4 plastic buckets filled to the top.

I fill this box with any potting mixture and garden soil of equal quantity. Add 1½ dessertspoons of lime. I usually toss this around for 10 to 14 days. Then add 1½ dessertspoons potash, 3 dessertspoons superphosphate, 3 dessertspoons blood and bone and the same measure of bone dust.

The easiest way to mix this thoroughly, is to tip it out onto a large piece of plastic or canvas, and then pull the corners into the middle alternately. I then add a margarine container, the 1 kilo size, of crushed eggshells, one container of soot and 2 containers of wood ash or fine charcoal, and mix it thoroughly. This mixture keeps carnations growing nicely. At budding stage I feed with Phostrogen or Aquasol. I use plastic pots and the eggshells allows air through the soil, keeping it sweet. Eggshells contain lime and that too is a bonus.

When potting carnations, make sure new roots are not exposed to the fertilised mixture; a light clean covering of sand may be needed. New roots need to grow into fertilised soil and if placed directly into this mixture they could burn which may retard the plant. More plants are killed by coming in contact with fertiliser or over fertilising, than by under fertilising.

Beware of heavy garden soil for potting carnations into. When the air cannot penetrate, the plant will wilt and suddenly die.

Do not fill the pots to the top with soil, leave about 3 cm for watering.

When planting the carnations, do not plant deeper than the ball of growing medium, or stem rot will result and the cultivar will die.

Watering of plants in pots can cause problems. Carnations do not like to be wet all the time, so the soil must be allowed to dry out occasionally. Continuous watering when the soil is already damp, will make it sour and carnations cannot thrive under these conditions. However, the larger the plant gets, the quicker it will use up water and therefore dry out. Carnations in pots need constant care.

If you need to leave your potted carnations without attention, due to holidays, etc., they can be left for three to four weeks in the open in a bed of seaweed. Place the pots on about 3-4 cm of seaweed and bring more around the outside of the pots, to about 3-4 cm from the top; almost all the pot is surrounded by seaweed.

Water well the morning you intend to leave, and unless a heat wave occurs, they will be quite happy for 3-4 weeks. The seaweed can later be used for a mulch around the garden. This is of course the fine black seaweed and not the ribbon type as I have described earlier. Any seaweed that is taken directly from the salt water must be hosed well first to get the salt out, but if it is picked up dry on the beach then it is usually all right to use immediately.

If there are slaters in the garden, a sprinkling of naphthalene flakes around the pots will discourage them.

If the weather is cool my pots might get watered only once a week, but always in the mornings. Those left in a seaweed mulch will survive for up to six weeks.

Deficiencies

Commercial growers have their fertilisers accurately measured. Many are grown hydroponically and only a breakdown in the system causes problems. Home growers rely on how a plant looks to measure its needs. There is no doubt that a healthy carnation is easy to pick out, but when it has deficiencies, it is not quite so easy.

Nitrogen
Plants show a yellowing and the number of shoots is reduced, with the leaves becoming narrower, shorter and straighter with weak flower stems. Too much nitrogen causes abnormally curved leaves that are dark green with possible leaf burn and root failing with yellowing of leaves and wilting.

Phosphorus
A shortage of phosphorus gives short pointed shoots with dark green foliage, older bottom leaves will die off and will continue until the deficiency is corrected.

Calcium
Calcium deficiency is unlikely if a pH level of 6–7 is maintained. Internode shortening and excessive side branching denote this problem though it occurs usually only in soilless medium.

Magnesium
Interveined chlorosis denotes this possibility, but generally it is not a problem unless too much potash has been applied. Yellowing of the leaves while the vein remains green, may be corrected with magnesium (Epsom salts) added to the liquid fertiliser.

Boron
Over-liming can cause boron deficiency, the leaves become twisted and yellow, top buds may be hollow and die. Upper nodes may produce excess growth. Tips of leaves may be dry, pale brown with a band of reddish purple.

Generally a good mixed fertiliser for home-grown carnations avoids these problems. Rose fertiliser has all the necessary requirements. Phostrogen, Aquasol and Thrive are fine if you like liquid fertilisers. I would recommend fortnightly applications of liquid fertiliser as soon as buds form, to keep the blooms healthy and in abundance. The number and quality of blooms depends on how the plant was fed.

Harvesting Blooms

One would think a chapter on harvesting flowers would be superfluous; even a child knows how to pick a flower. However, carnations need to be handled and treated with respect to get the longest possible life out of both the bloom and the plant.

Carnation blooms are best cut in the early morning, when the plants have had the cool of the night to rejuvenate. The stem will be crisp and brittle and break easily.

I rarely ever cut a carnation bloom as breaking off is far better. Stems break at the node. Cutting can leave a stub at the node, which in time can become infected with a fungus disease. Also rust and other diseases can be transmitted by cutting an infected plant and using the same implement to cut a bloom from a healthy plant, unless the cutting implement is dipped in a fungicide before moving on to the next bloom. This is worth avoiding for its nuisance value alone. When taking blooms, do not leave a long unsightly stub; take it back to a low healthy shoot to keep the plant compact.

It will be a few years yet before the new varieties become available. Since they are longer-lasting as cut flowers, the benefits will be enjoyed by commercial flower growers.

The first flowers from the early planting are usually formed on short stems, due to long daylight. Take care not to cut or break too low and damage vegetative shoots that produce the next crop. Stems with more than nine internodes may include vegetative shoots. Damaging these could shorten the life of production. Flowers may be picked when the outer petals are perpendicular to the calyx although I prefer to harvest when the bloom is almost fully out. Flowers will stop bursting open if placed in a cool room. Flower growers sometimes hold them for a week before marketing.

The lasting qualities of the blooms are affected by the time of harvesting, and whether the plant has been properly nourished. In the mornings the plant is fresher, and blooms picked then last longer. A bloom picked after a hot day wilts easily, although dipping the whole flower in water revives it a little.

As picking a flower cuts off its nutrient supply, a substitute is required. The flower stem needs to be placed in water as soon as possible after cutting, for delay is detrimental to the life span of the bloom. Carnations picked in mid-summer have a vase life of six days, and double that for cooler weather. However, a delay in getting cut flowers into water, say of two hours, will reduce their life by two days.

The quality of water is also important as water uptake through the stem decreases as salt content increases. I use only tank water for my carnation blooms; they last three to four days longer than in the scheme water containing fluoride, but I change the water every two days. Recutting the stem when changing the water will also increase flower longevity.

Commercial preservatives are available to lengthen the life of the flower, but I have never bothered. Sugar (about a teaspoon per vase) or citric acid (5 ml lemon juice per litre of water) are popular. Lemonade is very good as an aid in preserving the life of the flower. It is important to cut off the stem ends every two days as they rot and clog up preventing the flower from absorbing water.

There are many reasons why cut flowers do not last. Conditions detrimental to the life of cut flowers are the following: heated and stuffy rooms, where the temperatures drop overnight causing unnatural conditions; the presence of smoke, kerosene and gas heaters; being near fruit, especially apples; failure to immediately remove any dead flowers from a vase.

Vases and bowls must be thoroughly clean before use as accumulated dirt will cause water to become stale. Needle and pin holders can be cleaned with a stiff brush. Do not leave any leaves submerged in water as they quickly decay making the water sour. Never pack flowers tightly in a vase as the stems need room to breathe, and of course never place the vase in sunlight.

Sweet peas are not good for the life of other flowers when they are mixed in a vase as they sap the life out of them.

I always wear jeans or slacks made of a close weave material when harvesting blooms. Carnation stems are very brittle and can snap off when brushed with the hem of a skirt. Lace edges on a petticoat or slip are very hazardous, catching in buds as you walk past or bend to pick a bloom. It is very disappointing to find a special bud snapped off by a dangling thread from a skirt hem; you will never notice it until too late.

I rang one grower in Perth, asking if I could see his garden; he is noted for his prize blooms in all the agricultural and horticultural shows. He was very noncommital, but gave me the address and a time to visit.

When I arrived his first words were, 'So you know carnations then'.

My surprised reply was a doubtful, 'Yes, a bit'.

He said, 'You know, if you had been wearing a skirt, you would have got no further than the gate'.

I spent a very pleasant two hours with this gentleman, exchanging views. His current interest was in developing a carnation that did not require the time-consuming operation of disbudding. This problem is now being experimented on in Europe.

Shows and Showing

Every time I went to the local agricultural and horticultural show, the carnation display was my first stop.

I looked at one of the blooms and thought 'mine are as good as that'. Well I happened to express my thoughts out loud, not realising anyone was near. The president of the society introduced herself and informed me, she expected to see some late entries from me the following morning before 9 a.m.; judging was to be at 11 a.m.

The morning was a revelation.

Not knowing how to exhibit anything, I took a variety of flowers down to the pavilion, unsure of which category they came under.

Other exhibitors were working at displaying their own flowers, and were quick with advice and help. I was amazed at the help and hints from people I was competing with. It was more like a group eager to exchange information.

I did not take any prizes for my carnations, though I did take three prizes in other categories. What I thought was a good carnation was nothing more than personal preference, a nice bloom but unable to amass enough points. The competition was very keen and it was easy to see the near perfection of other entries. However, it was a worthwhile learning period, particularly as other growers were willing to advise on points procedures for judging.

There are differing views on getting your blooms ready for showing. Flowers grown on benches are allowed to hang over naturally, this stops the outer petals from curling.

I did see a plant that had been stopped to create 15 flower stalks. These were all allowed to hang naturally. The outer blooms were slightly discoloured by splashes from the ground, but the rest were perfect, with no outer petals curved at all.

A protective stand with a flower pot covering as described on page 28 will stop outer petals curling and give perfect results.

Show Points

The calyx must be round and not split, firm and not soft, well filled.
The bloom should rise to one and one-third the height of the calyx.
The bloom should have even-sized petals, smooth, round and unblemished.
The outer petals should be firm and not curled down.
The colour should be clear without fading.
The stem should be erect, strong, whippy and not thick.
Fragrance is always a strong point winner.
Foliage must be of good colour, free of insect damage or infection.
Do take good care of blooms when transporting them to a show, as they are easy to damage in transit, making them quite useless for transporting.

Judges vary a little in awarding points but generally they follow the same pattern:

Condition—3
Form of flower—3
Stem—3
Calyx—3
Substance—3
Fragrance—3
Colour—2

These categories make a total of 20 points.

Handy Hints

For information and advice on all your gardening problems, your local horticultural society is a good place to start. New members are welcomed and many useful titbits of practical information are exchanged among members.

I was advised to give my carnations a sprinkle of magnesium sulphate (Epsom salts) when I remarked that a couple of plants were stunted with thick short pale-coloured stems; it worked!

Horses like to eat carnation plants, so your old plants can be fed to the horses if any are around. Please make sure the carnations have not been sprayed tor the previous four weeks; it would not be nice to give the horses a headache.

Do not grow your carnations in diffused light or shade as they will be weak and of poor colour.

Slaters do not like naphthalene so, if you have a picket fence, sprinkle with naphthalene flakes which are available at any supermarket. Remember that naphthalene is poisonous to small children.

Carnations planted in soil where you have grown hyacinths, will die. The reverse is also true: planting hyacinths where you had carnations growing will give the same result.

Banana skins are rich in sulphur, magnesium, sodium, calcium and phosphates: don't waste them, scratch them into topsoil around rose bushes or geraniums or feed them to staghorn and elkhorn ferns.

Lizards in the garden are not a pest, they eat snails, grasshoppers and beetles.

Marigolds are useful to have in the garden, especially the African types; pests don't like them.

Don't kill a dragonfly, it's probably doing you a service catching garden pests.

Lacewings are small green insects with four gauzy wings and golden eyes, often seen pottering around an outside light; they eat aphids, caterpillars and mealy bugs.

Ladybirds with their bright coat of red, yellow or orange with black spots will be hard at work eating your aphids.

When carnations are staked, they must have room for air to circulate, or rust and wilt will attack.

A carnation takes up to 45 square centimetres of space. Plants must be kept clean and well fed.

The record for a standard carnation is 42 blooms at the same time on one plant. This was achieved by stopping until sufficient flower stalks formed, and fed each week. In this case, the plant would not be staked as the flowers would hold each other up.

A fertiliser mix of nitrogen, phosphorous and potassium, N.P.K. rating 5:6:5 is ideal.

The amount of light aids blooms in opening. Short days delay flowering but make for longer stems and slightly larger flowers with more lateral growth. Long daylight brings quick results.

Avoid planting carnations in the same place every year, a two- to three-year break is required to keep diseases under control.

Destroy old plantings, do not put in the compost.

Prepare the ground early to reduce undecomposed plant debris.

Avoid growing carnations with statice, gypsophila, hyacinths or bougainvillea.

Propagate only from healthy plants.

Do not plant too deeply, or stem rot may occur.

Keep leaves dry whenever possible to discourage rust.

Hygienic conditions in handling, pruning and propagation discourages disease.

Secateurs can be sterilised in household chlorine bleach diluted one part to three parts of water.

Beds must be free-draining for good growth.

There is no reason why Garden Club members cannot get together with other clubs, and order blocks of 50 plants of the one variety, to be split up among them. It is too time-consuming for big nurseries with the best stock to fiddle around with small orders.

Carnations are often referred to as the buttonholes of the world, and are second in popularity to the rose worldwide.

Early botanists gave the name *Dianthus caryophyllus* to the dianthus because it smelled a little like cloves. *Caryophyllus* was the old name for cloves. The Romans knew the carnation well and gave it the name *carnatio*, which is Latin for 'fleshy'. In those days they were pink or reddish pink.

Scarlet carnation (of the dianthus family) was adopted by legislative action in February 1904 as the State flower of Ohio. U.S.A.

Carnation Marmalade

Carnations have always been grown in gardens for their colour and perfume, but were included in old herb gardens for making marmalade. I have never tried it, but the recipe is as follows:

Take half a pound of sugar, a cup of water and half a pound of fresh red carnations. Crush the carnation tops with a mortar. Put the sugar and water in a saucepan and boil to a syrup, adding crushed carnations. Boil very slowly until they pulp. Stir well and pour into small jars when set.

Named Carnations

At times we see a carnation of the same colouring, but with a different name to the one we have at home. There are hundreds of carnations available in Australia, as well as many propagators, commercial and hobbyist, so it stands to reason there will be considerable similarity in colour and stature of many blooms.

Some plants I have had for 20 years have gone. Many have died through neglect. Others died in a heat wave, while I was away. Genuine carnation fanciers keep in contact seeking old stock to rejuvenate. The reliable, hardy, prolific old faithfuls, are unavailable on today's market. The new modern plants are kept for only a few seasons, then some new strain takes its place.

'Flamingo' in the Avonmore carnations is a beautiful pink with yellow shadings, while 'Flamingo' in Sims carnations is flamingo pink.

'Candy' in the Avonmore carnation range is a lovely soft candy pink with a large bloom and strong stem. Then there are the new Selecta Klemm varieties with their 'Candy' range.

Most of us buy a plant when we see one that we are attracted to; this is the best and safest way and the least confusing. Someone may be selling a species they have grown for many years and which has long been forgotten by commercial growers.

Choosing your carnation plants is strictly a matter of preference. Many people like the Perpetual Flowering varieties but do not want to spend the time looking after them, and they do need more attention than any others. Border carnations will give fine displays for less work, and some can be kept flowering all year, with slightly smaller blooms and shorter stems. Spray, field and seed carnations can be planted and let flower at will.

While Avonmore has had the same varieties for many years, Sims have genetically engineered better plants, with the colours much the same. Kooij has a range of good quality plants, with a variety of colours. All these are available to the general public, as are some miniatures. It's worth shopping around to get the best.

Standard or Perpetual Flowering Varieties

'**Alice**' Clear yellow with some fine red markings; renowned for production and quality.

'**Aliseo**' New cerise, good production, tolerant.

'**Amethyst**' Amethyst-toned, good blooms, plant inclined to go straggly (Plate 1)

'**Anne Marie**' Bright red with fine white stripe and edges, strong grower, large blooms.

'**Arevalo**' Deep purple with lavender edges, strong stems. (Plate 15)

'**Astor**' Red hybrid, fast grower with excellent qualities.

'**Aurigo**' Mid-pink, strong growth with good vase life.

'**Berlina**' Beautiful soft pink, perfect bloom.

'**Bogota**' Pure white with quality blooms.

'**Borello**' Yellow, of good quality, strong stems.

'**Buggio**' Gold with pink fleck. Large bloom, high quality with no splitting.

'**Bushfire**' Pale orange splashed with turkey red, open bloom.

'**Candy**' Klemm 'Candy' is a yellow with pink flecks. Avonmore 'Candy' is soft pink (Plate 16)

'**Carla**' Orange with good growth and colour.

'**Cantalupo**' Red, high production. strong stems.

'**Carola**' Light lavender, quality blooms.

'**Charlotte**' White with red edge, fast grower, strong plant.

'**Clara**' Porcelain pink, fast strong grower.

'**Dark Pierrot**' Deep lilac with purple edge. (Plate 27)

'**Dedalo**' Orange with red stripe. Strong grower.

'**Delphi**' White, large bloom, strong stem. (Plate 28)

'**Dona**' Cerise pink, picot-edged, uniform bloom. (Plate 29)

'**Duberry**' Tall rose, good stem, grows well. (Plate 2)

'**Dusty Pink**' Pale pink, uniform bloom.

'**Effi**' Pale mauve, strong stems.

'**Erica**' White with red fleck, fast grower.

'**Fiona**' Strawberry pink, lovely bright colour, large blooms strong stems. (Plate 17)

'**Flair**' New lilac, smooth-edged petals.

'**Flamingo**' Sims 'Flamingo' is dark pink. Avonmore 'Flamingo' is pink with yellow markings (Plate 18)

'**Francesco**' Red that grows fast with good blooms.

'**Gala**' Large pale pink, fringed edge. (Plate 32)

'**Gatsby**' Produces large white blooms on strong stems.

'**Gigi**' Red, high producer of medium-size flowers.

'**Ginevra**' Light pink, fast grower, quality blooms.

'**Harvest Moon**' Yellow with pink stripe.

'**Havana**' Lemon with pale mauve edge.

'**Helios**' Dark cerise, lovely uniform bloom.

'**Iberia**' Bright yellow with pencilled red edge, fast strong grower.

'**Iceberg**' White, tall strong plant.

'**Incas**' Bright yellow with red edge, strong uniform bloom.

'**Indios**' Red, high producer, no splitting.

'**Isac**' Bright yellow, tall strong growth.

'**Ivonne**' Large, yellow blooms with fine red edge, high producer.

'**Ivonne Orange**' Orange with red edge.

'**Izeraeli**' Pale mauve, long strong stems. (Plate 33)

'**Izmir**' Large frosted mauve, strong plant. (Plate 34)

'**Kaly**' Pure white, few splits, high production.

'**Kinko**' Yellow on strong stems, uniform bloom.

'**Koranja**' Tangerine, strong grower, popular.

'**Kristina**' Light pink pencilled garnet, fast grower high producer. (Plate 36)

'**Laddie**' Pastel pink, old favourite.

'**Laika**' White with red stripe, large bloom, productive plant. (Plate 4)

'**Las Palmas**' Sims new yellow, large strong bloom. (Plate 37)

'**Laurella**' Cyclamen, fast grower, high producer. (Plate 38)

'**Lavender Lace**' Bright lavender, prolific grower, good perfume (Plate 5)

'**Liberty**' Soft yellow, strong prolific grower. (Plate 39)

'**Lisboa**' White with maroon splash, quality plant. (Plate 40)

'**Lolita**' Geranium-red centre with wide white edge. (Plate 19)

'**Lyndal**' Orchid pink with wide white edge. (Plate 20).

'**Madeline**' Deep ruby red with light frosted edge, lovely perfume. (Plate 21)

'**Malta**' Salmon pink, prolific, fast grower.

'**Malaga**' Special orange. This is a top carnation, large bloom, prolific. (Plate 41)

'**Manon**' Deep pink, high yields during summer months, fast growth.

'**Master**' Bright red, fast growth, quality bloom. (Plate 42)

'**Miledy**' Large bright pink, top bloom, strong stems.

'**Miledy Brilliant**' Brilliant pink, large bloom.

'**Minerva**' Deep purple with white fringed edge, large blooms.

'**Nelson**' Red, good colour, uniform bloom. (Plate 45)

'**Nicol**' Cerise centre, pale pink edge, large bloom, eye-catching.

'**Nordika**' White, good quality, fast growth.

'**Opal**' Pale yellow with mauve edge, lovely soft colouring, sensitive to cold. (Plate 22)

'**Orange Magic**' Large bright orange, strong stem. (Plate 46)

'**Orchard Beauty**' Lavender, large bloom long stems. (Plate 23)

'**Oriana**' Bright pink, grows fast, nice bloom.

'**Osaka**' Light pink, paler edge.

'**Pallas**' Brilliant yellow, uniform bloom.

'Paola' Bright pink, high producer, no splitting.

'Pax' Cream, one of the few creams available.

'Pierrot' Light pink with purple edge, Large bloom on strong stem.

'Pikes Peak Frosted' Strawberry with white markings.

'Pink Dona' Pale pink, picot edge.

'Pink Ice' Ruffled pink, paling to the edge, large bloom. (Plate 6)

'Pink Mist' Blushing pink, uniform bloom.

'Pontiac' Bright yellow, purple edge. Large blooms, prolific.

'Prado' Light green, smooth-edged petals. (Plate 47)

'President' Violet with paler edge, quality plant.

'Purple Rendevous' Large purple, strong grower, smooth-edged petals (Plate 49)

'Ramona' Pale pink, large uniform bloom.

'Raggio De Sole' Orange, strong grower, quality bloom. (Plate 50)

'Red Diamond' White ground with fine red stripe, large bloom, strong stem (Plates 7–9)

'Rendevous' Cream white with crimson edge, top quality bloom, high producer. (cover plate)

'Rimini' Bright red, fast strong growth.

'Roderigas' Deep pink with pale edge, beautiful large bloom, on strong stem. (Plate 51)

'Roma' Cream, strong growth with few splits.

'Rosette' Brilliant phlox pink, full flower, strong stem. (Plate 24)

'Rose Carola' Salmon pink, strong reliable plant.

'Safari' Frosted purple with large flower on tall stem, very popular. (Plate 25)

'Salamanca' Yellow, large bloom, tall stem. (Plate 52)

'Sally' Bright yellow with pink splashes, high production. (Plate 26)

'Salome' Red, strong stem, few splits.

'Samur' Light pink, maroon edge, strong high-producing plant, top quality. (Plate 53)

'Samur, Sport of' To be registered. (Plate 54)

'Scania' Light red, popular for its long stem.

'Solar' Orange with red stripes. Strong growth, productive.

'Sonsara' White, very high producer, good quality bloom.

'Starry' Yellow, strong bloom, tall stem.

'Storm' Pansy-mauve petal, base rose-toned, large bloom strong stem. (Plate 10)

'Sugar' Delicate light pink, strong plant. (Plate 56)

'Sydney Blue' Mauve to purple with paler fringed edge, an old one still available occasionally.

'Tahiti' Bright yellow, fast growth, high producer.

'Tangerine' Orange with tangerine stripe, large bloom. (Plate 11)

'Telstar' Yellow with red stripe, tall stem. (Plate 12)

'Tigre' Yellow with purple stripe and edge. (Plate 13)

'Totem' Vivid red stripe on salmon pink background, large bloom.

'**Tundra**' Yellow with light red edge, beautiful strong grower. (Plate 59)

'**Uniko**' Pink with pale edge, large uniform bloom on strong stem.

'**Venere**' Pale lilac with fringed edge. Lovely large bloom on strong stem.

'**Venus**' Light pink, smooth round petals.

'**Verona**' Gold, high production.

'**Vienna**' Pink, maroon fringe stripe, productive (Plate 60)

'**Virginie**' White, high producer of quality blooms. (Plate 61)

'**Vivianne**' Pink, strong plant producing nice blooms.

'**White Dutch**' Standard white.

'**White Candy**' High yield of quality blooms.

'**White Ibizia**' Fast growth , strong stem.

'**Zamora**' Quality pink, large full flower. (Plate 14)

'**Ziggy**' Cream, fringed petals, very effective.

Borders and Pinks

Borders and Pinks have shorter stem growth than Standard carnations. They are easier to grow as they require less attention. A garden bordered with Pinks is very effective. A wide range of colours are available.

*Indicates results of cross- pollination by small breeders.

'**Bonney**' Yellow with dark pink edge and fleck. Summer flowering.

'**Clare**' White ground with rose pink markings.

'**Doris**' Salmon pink with azalea pink eye.

'**Jon Cleary**' White with purple edge, very hardy, used for cross-pollination. (Plate 3)

'**Joy**' Yellow, slight pink fleck.

* '**Kiwi Gem**' White with maroon eye, charming bloom. (Plate 35)

* '**Monica**' Yellow with burgundy edge and fleck.

'**Pink Pearl**' Smooth, uniform open bloom.

* '**Prissi Anne**' Yellow with fringed red edge. (Plate 48)

'**Purple Haze**' Cream with purple stripes.

'**Robin**' White with deep crimson edge and splash.

★ '**Terry Billings**' Top Border carnation. Yellow with bright red edge. (Plate 58)

★ '**T.S. Cutler**' Beautiful colour, white with lavender edge and stripe.

Florini and Sprays.

There are as many Florini and Spray carnations available now as there are Standards. It would be impossible to list them all, as all growers carry stock. This list will be a mere fraction of what the top growers have stocked recently, and to give an idea of the large range available.

'**Alicetta**' Yellow with deep pink edge.

'**Alister**' Bright red, good growth and production.

'**Boreal**' Lavender, fast grower.

'**Brio**' Bright pink. (Plate 31)

'**Cartouche**' Golden yellow.

'**Cotillon**' Pink stripe.

'**Exquisite**' White edge, purple heart.(Plate 31)

'**Furore**' Bright orange.

'**Green Castle**' Light green, deeper centre.

'**Iceland**' Cream, strong growth.

'**Kappa**' Bright pink with wide light pink edge.

'**Lara**' White, red stripe.

'**Marcena**' Light orange, pencilled red stripe.

'**Minstral. Florini.**' Large bright pink, pale edge.

'**Mirna**' Bright yellow.

'**Monica**' Brilliant violet.

'**Nita**' White, wide crimson edge.

'**Ondelia**' Cherry , fast growth.

'**Regis**' White, red edge

'**Rony**' Deep red.

'**Taiga**' Yellow with red stripe. (Plate 57)

'**Tangerine**' Yellow ground with thick tangerine edge and splash. (Plate 11)

'**Target**' Orange with deep orange stripe.

'**Tip Top**' Orange with red stripe.

'**Virgo**' Light cream.

'**White Lili Anne**' White strong growth.

'**Zagor, Florini.**' Burgundy, productive plant. (Plate 62)

Micro Carnations (Dwarf Sprays)

'Echo' Two-toned pink. (Plate 30)

'Lima' Bright pink.

'Roland' Cerise, very prolific. (Plate 30)

'Orca' White with purple edge.

'Pampa' Cerise.

'Unesco' Cream with pink edge. (Plate 30)

Chinesini

'Lulu' Comes in pink, white and cerise.

'Mei Bao' (Plate 43)
'Mei Fu' (Plate 44)

Gipsy

Gipsy is a new breed of carnation, growing to a metre tall, with a bloom similar to a Sweet William. These also are still under patent.

'Gipsy' Plain colours are white, lilac, dark pink and red.
'Giant Gipsy' Lilac.

'Sunset Gipsy' Tangerine red.
'Sparkling Gipsy' Lilac with white centre.

Even as these are being written up, someone will find they have a flower of a different colour from the mother plant, and will be perfecting that 'sport' for further production. New types and colours are being grown every year, and with the great number of commercial and private growers in Australia, it would be impossible to keep track of all the new ones being introduced.

What's New

New breeders in the last eight to ten years have made a great impact on the varieties available. Names like Briers, Kooij, Klemm, Zonen, Van Staavern, West-stek, Lek, Hilverda are just a few of the names on the lists of registered stock. As with the newer Sims carnations, all these plants are now of top quality, in that they are better producers, with little or no tendency to split. The perfume quality has also been improved, with buyers' demands catered for. Flowers are now big business.

Spray carnations have now gained in popularity in Australia. They are easy to grow, give a lovely display, and need less attention than the Standard variety. Sprays have a free-branching growth pattern, with many small blooms per stem. I have had 'Roland', a plain cerise spray with 25 buds on the one stem. As one bloom fades I pinch it out and allow the next bud to burst open. To nip out the first terminal bud will allow a spray to branch out, but it may be treated as a Standard carnation to grow one larger bloom, if required.

Mini (dwarf), Sprays, Micro (the size of a 50-cent piece), Mini Micro (the size of 10 cents) and Chinesini are all proving popular in floral combinations. These high-yielding carnations with petite forms require a minimum of labour.

Gipsy is a new carnation with a flower head like Sweet William, yet they grow a metre high and are quite bushy. Colours are mostly plain.

One grower in Victoria has gone over to growing only the 'Lulu' variety, due to its popularity with florists.

'Lulu' is a smooth-edged, beautifully formed carnation with more petals than a spray. It looks like a half size Standard. It has one or two buds per stem, but many stems per plant, making for much less labour. The colours are plain.

It is to be hoped a new breeder in Victoria will soon have some of his English pinks, borders and dianthus available. Paul Rumkorf has not gone commercial yet, but his experiments are well worth mentioning. I have taken a few photos of his new varieties; I found them most interesting. Although the blooms are in the smaller scale they are nonetheless worth mentioning for their variety of colour, and the perfume. His thick border of English pinks was beautiful and many pinks have vase length stems.

Then of course we get the field carnations, which are the blooms you see in bunches at the supermarket, or on the roadside stalls.

All new carnations will have a royalty of up to 10 cents per plant, which is added to the cost for the buyer. This royalty helps in the massive cost of tissue culture, quarantine fees and upkeep.

Many of these plants will become free of royalties and be available to the general public. 'Raggio De Sole', 'Laika' and 'Manon' are a few, while other old-time favourites like 'Orchid Beauty' and the best of Sims are still grown. Chinesini, Gipsy and Micro will be unavailable for a few years yet.

Sometimes a plant will grow a bloom of a different colour and this is referred to as a mutation, or a renegade bloom. Should the grower take a cutting from this flower stalk and reproduce the mutation, that mutation is still the property of the breeder of the original plant, if it is under patent. To reproduce this renegade bloom, the grower must notify the breeder who has the right of ownership of the mutation. He will then perfect it and register it with a name, referring to it as a sport of the original plant.

I have recently visited large carnation farms in South Australia, Victoria and Queensland. The scale of operations is overwhelming, with hothouses in all directions full of continuous rows of carnations grown on benches or in the ground. One hothouse has 50 benches topped with trays of cuttings, one million per tray, all rooted and ready for sale. Each tray had cuttings from only one variety. It was shown how much easier it is to sell in blocks of 50 plants, one square lifted out with the required number already assured. To grow for individual orders would upset the system considerably, as they would need to be propagated elsewhere.

The large variety of carnations now being grown has mushroomed over the last few years. Baguleys list 13 different groups in their brochures. With different groups of Standards and Sprays, some under patent, to English pinks, Field, Pots, Micro, Chinesini and Gipsy. Most farms grow carnations in at least six varieties, keeping four to fifteen of the most saleable varieties.

When you see the scope of a large commercial farm, where everything is done in clinical conditions, it does not seem in any way to relate to the home gardener. Everyone here is too busy to admire the exquisite blooms; the scene is impersonal, high technology production. When a carnation does not meet the high standard required (for instance, in one case it was pointed out that all the petals were not uniform), then that variety is discarded and unceremoniously dumped.

Big places face enormous costs to keep their farms free of disease. Visitors are rarely allowed into the propagating sheds, as most work is done under laboratory conditions, where workers wear sterilised boots. Sheds are constructed not only for temperature control, but to ensure no bugs from outside can enter.

These large farms may be required to pay up-front a sum of $2000 to $6000 (depending on the number of hothouses they have) to the Agricultural Department for testing, to get a quarantine certificate stating they are pest-free.

When this money runs out, then a fee of $86 per test may need to be paid. Then a quarantine officer may arrive to inspect the plants every 8-12 weeks; the cost is generally $80 for each visit.

The Department of Agriculture tests for viruses and fungal diseases. Quarantine officers look for bugs and insects. Because of the western flower thrip, said to be in all states except Victoria and Tasmania, quarantine officers inspect all nurseries exporting plant material. For this reason it is uneconomical to order less than 1000 plants, as a quarantine fee of $80 may be incurred.

This is some of the cost the general public would not be aware of, and the reason why nurseries with the best stock are reluctant to sell in small quantities. If this idea of selling plants in six-packs through the supermarkets comes to fruition, it will be a big boost for home growers.

I was well received at all places I visited. Growers were interested in what I was doing, many not wanting to be mentioned as they did not cater for small orders. I would advise buyers to ring around to find a nursery willing to propagate an order; there are a few. There will generally be a four- to six-week delay before your plants are ready.

If you wish to visit a carnation farm, ring first to make an appointment. Some farms conduct bus tours, which are usually full of overseas tourists. On a previous occasion I ran into a group of Japanese business men, which gave me little chance of asking questions.

I love the packing sheds, filled with fragrance and colour, where hundreds of perfect blooms are boxed, in boxes labelled in Japanese, Dutch, German, French and English ready for transport. A less than perfect carnation is squashed and dropped in the bin, as there are hundreds of better ones on the bench. A man fills a trolley with the completed boxes and wheels them into the cool room. There is no time for me, I am unsupervised, can look, not touch. I am pleased with the visit, but glad to get back to the smallness of my own garden and individuality.

The clinical procedures of a carnation farm would put any home gardener to shame. There is no sentiment there; it's a case of produce top quality or we're not interested. One thing I did learn, was that all growers claimed to be still learning and were interested in any information available.

I cannot speak too highly of Graeme Guy, the plant pathologist at Baguleys, in Victoria. Graeme gave me a lot of his time and much information on modern techniques, to which I would otherwise not have had access.

Many of the plants are now free of patents and Kooij have released quite a few of theirs. I did notice some of the new carnations look the same as the old ones, but the new breed will be stronger, less likely to split, be more disease-resistant, have better perfume and have fewer buds per stem, to cut down on the disbudding. The future for carnations looks promising, I look forward to acquiring some of the new beautiful varieties.

I wrote to seventeen carnation farms, before setting out on this quest. Fifteen replied. Some no longer grew carnations; those who did sent their brochure, with lists of what was available. Most places I visited, I did so without an appointment as I had no set schedule, and no knowledge of the time they had to spare me. I had an overall time limit of ten weeks. Many I did not get time to visit, only because of travelling time.

Those seeking quality plants will find some advertised in gardening magazines, or try some of the places I have mentioned. Prices will vary with different growers, but there is value in good quality plants, and quality plants produce top blooms.

Season's Jobs

Winter

Dead and old leaves and any broken or damaged branches should be removed, and weeds eliminated.

Mid to late winter is the best time to start propagating, if a hot house or sheltered area is available.

Flowering plants will benefit from a light dressing of chalk lime. Occasional spraying for aphid and greenfly may be necessary.

If carnations are kept in pots, now is the time to get potting mixes ready in advance.

Check to see if you have enough insecticide for later requirements.

Commence preparation of beds for planting when propagated shoots are ready.

Spring

New plants will be coming onto the market, especially in the supermarkets, in September–October; consider updating your stock. These will be of popular colours, any special named varieties will have to be ordered through your local nurseries.

Flowering plants can now have a light dressing of blood and bone, and liquid fertiliser such as Aquasol, Phostrogen or Nitrosol.

Potted plants may need to be stopped and some will be ready to plant out.

Watch out for infestations of red mite and other pests.

Growth of the plants will be rapid now, so regular feeding will be necessary for a continuation of good flowers. Also a time for disbudding.

There will be plenty of healthy new shoots for propagating new plants if needed. These can be put beside the mother plant, or in the garden at an undisturbed spot, if starting boxes are not on hand.

Watch out for rust and signs of wilt; use a fungicide spray before they occur. Do not overwater, there could still be enough dew at night to keep the plants damp enough. Allow to dry out occasionally, it helps to control rust and wilt.

Summer

Plants are likely to need some support now, especially if in pots.

Do not let the garden become too dry; a mulch is advisable to conserve moisture and prevent burn when the hot sun reflects back off the ground.

General work of feeding, spraying, disbudding, watering and stopping where required.

Potted plants that have flowered indoors may now be planted in the garden; give some shelter from full sun for a few days.

Enjoy your flowers, there should be plenty.

Autumn

Rust may be noticed now and any plant with wilt or mildew should be burned.

Plants with rust can be cut back to two healthy shoots and sprayed with Benlate. Cut back severely only where necessary.

Potted plants that are cut back now should flower in winter, if kept protected from the cold.

This is a good time to wash and sterilise all pots not in use for later.

Generally clean up the area and check on requirements for next season.

Cultivar Index

(numbers in **bold** refer to colour plates.)

General Index